Waists & Waistbands

skills institute press

Distributed By
Fox Chapel Publishing

FOX CHAPEL
PUBLISHING

A DIRECTORY OF DESIGN DETAILS AND TECHNIQUES

© 2011 by Skills Institute Press LLC
"Select-n-Stitch Fashion Elements" series trademark of Skills Institute Press
Published and distributed in North America by Fox Chapel Publishing Company, Inc.,
East Petersburg, PA.

Waists & Waistbands is an original work, first published in 2011.

Portions of text and art previously published by and reproduced under license with
Direct Holdings Americas Inc.

ISBN 978-1-56523-555-7

Library of Congress Cataloging-in-Publication Data

Waists & waistbands. -- First.
    pages cm. -- (Select-n-Stitch Fashion Elements)
  Includes index.
  ISBN 978-1-56523-555-7
  1. Waists (Clothing) 2. Waistbands. I. Fox Chapel Publishing. II. Title: Waists and
waistbands.
  TT560.W345 2011
  646.2--dc22
                                2010048407

To learn more about the other great books from Fox Chapel Publishing,
or to find a retailer near you, call toll-free 800-457-9112 or visit us at
www.FoxChapelPublishing.com.

Note to Authors: We are always looking for talented authors to write new books.
Please send a brief letter describing your idea to
Acquisition Editor, 1970 Broad Street, East Petersburg, PA 17520.

Printed in China
First printing: July 2011

Table of Contents

Welcome to
Select-n-Stitch FASHION ELEMENTS

Waists
& Waistbands

Whether you're sewing tailored trousers or a casual dress, having the right instructions can make a difference in the success of a garment. With step-by-step illustrations and thorough instructions, Select-n-Stitch gives you the in-depth information you need to learn or refine a technique and sew garments successfully the first time.

Use the contents page and Select-n-Stitch guides to find common fashion elements, such as a trouser waistband, drawstring waist, or peplum, and then flip to the detailed instructions to learn the best methods for constructing them. Whether you're using commercial patterns, modifying patterns, or mixing and matching to make your own creation, use these instructions to complete your sewing projects beautifully.

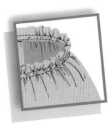

Waistbands for Pants & Skirts,
page 8

Waistbands are one of the fundamental elements of pants, shorts, and skirts. Learn the best methods to form common waistband designs so they fit, lie flat, and look great.

Dress Waists, page 58

The best dresses combine a fitted top and body-skimming bottom into a pretty, pleasing whole. Simple techniques ensure the pieces join smoothly at the waist and hang straight.

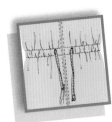

Waistbands for Jackets, page 90

Create a comfortable, flattering fit by applying waistband techniques to athletic or outdoor gear, sweaters, and other tops.

Fitting New & Existing Garments, page 108

Whether it's trousers you made or a pair you bought, don't settle for a less-than-perfect fit. These quick tips will help you adjust the waistband so it's flat, flattering, and comfortable.

Adjusting Patterns, page 122

Take the time to fit a pattern once, and then make stylish and appealing garments every time you sew. Learn how to adjust commercial patterns so they fit your body.

Buttons & Buttonholes, page 158

Buttons are like jewelry for clothes. Learn how to choose, place, size, and sew buttons, and sew strong, attractive buttonholes.

Basic Stitches, page 164

Not sure what an overcast stitch or slip stitch looks like? Find straightforward instructions for key stitches.

Select-n-Stitch Waistbands for Pants & Skirts

Waistbands are one of the fundamental elements of pants, shorts, and skirts. Learn the best methods to form common waistband designs so they fit, lie flat, and look great.

Basic Elastic Waistband,
page 10

Drawstring Waist,
page 22

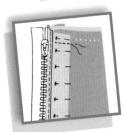

Lapped Zipper,
page 26

Women's Fly-Front Zipper,

Men's Fly-Front Zipper,

Trouser Waistband,

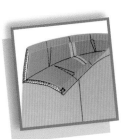

Waist with Ribbon Facing,

Basic Elastic Waistband
Basic waistband without a header

1a. To determine the best depth for the casing, measure the width of the elastic you plan to use and add ¼ inch for clearance and ⅜ inch for the seam allowance. The total of these three figures will give you the proper depth.

2a. Form a casing by folding the top edge of the skirt over toward the wrong side by the amount determined in Step 1a.

3a. Pin along the fold at 1-inch intervals. Baste and remove the pins.

4a. Turn under the free edge of the casing ⅜ inch, pinning at 1-inch intervals as you go. Baste this edge to the skirt leaving an open space wide enough to insert the elastic. Remove the pins.

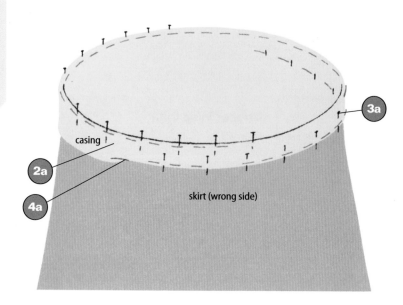

casing

skirt (wrong side)

5a. Machine stitch around the top edge of the waist ⅛ inch in from the edge. Remove the basting.

6a. Machine stitch around the bottom edge of the casing ⅛ inch from the edge, leaving open the space where the elastic will be inserted. Remove the basting. Skip to Step 7b.

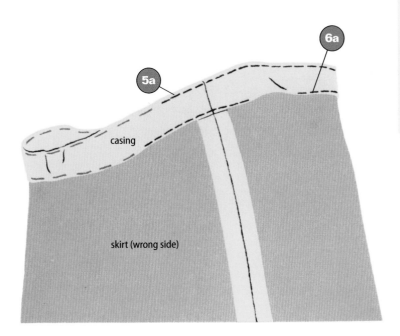

casing

skirt (wrong side)

Basic Elastic Waistband
Basic waistband with a header

1b. Cut the garment sections following your pattern instructions, but make sure to provide a 1½-inch allowance for the waistband casing. Then assemble the garment, stitching all seams closed up to the waistline edge. Press open the seams.

2b. Turn the garment right side out.

3b. Fold the waistline edge of the garment to the wrong side ¼ inch and press. Then fold along the casing fold line and press.

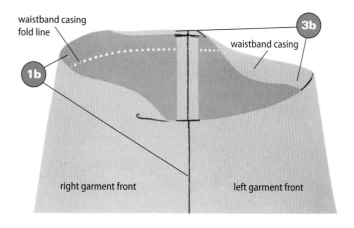

waistband casing fold line

3b

waistband casing

1b

right garment front

left garment front

4b. Pin the waistband casing to the garment, inserting the pins from the wrong side of the garment.

5b. Sewing from the wrong side of the garment, machine stitch ⅛ inch from the inner edge of the casing. At the center back, leave an unstitched opening of about 1½ inches for inserting the elastic. Remove the pins.

6b. Make a second line of machine stitching ⅜ inch above the first one. Stitch completely around the garment without leaving an opening.

7b. Cut a piece of ¼-inch-wide elastic, or the width to fit your casing, ½ inch longer than your waistline. Attach a safety pin to one end. Push that end of the elastic into the opening in the lower edge of the casing; thread the elastic through the casing.

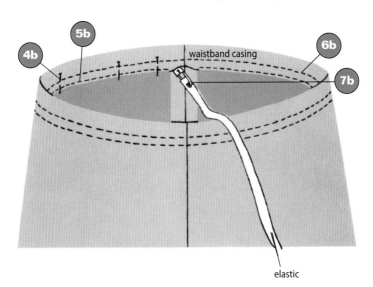

waistband casing

elastic

Basic Elastic Waistband
Basic waistband with a header

8b. After the elastic has been pulled through the casing, remove the safety pin. Lap the ends by ½ inch and join them with a line of machine zigzag stitches. Stitch forward and then back for extra strength.

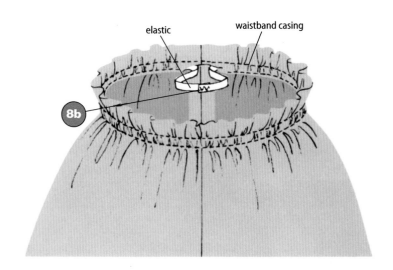

elastic

waistband casing

8b

9b. Pull on the waistband so that the ends of the elastic disappear into the casing.

10b. Close the opening through which the elastic was inserted with machine stitching. Then adjust the fullness evenly around the waistline.

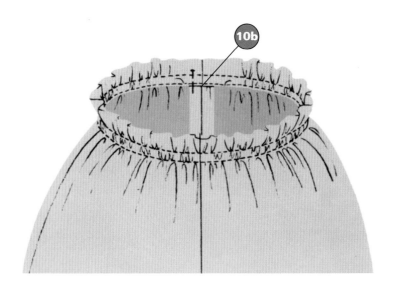

Basic Elastic Waistband

Basic waistband with alternate casing

1c. Cut the garment sections following your pattern instructions, but make sure to provide a 1¼-inch allowance for the waistband casing. Then assemble the garment, stitching all seams closed up to the waistline edge. Press open the seams.

2c. Turn the garment right side out.

3c. Sewing from the wrong side of the garment, finish the raw waistline edge with a line of machine zigzag stitches.

4c. Insert a pin along the casing fold line at a seam. Pin from the wrong side of the garment. Then insert three additional pins along the fold line, dividing the waistline into four equal parts.

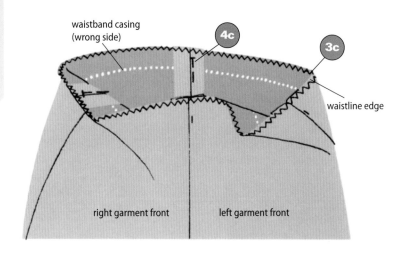

waistband casing
(wrong side)

4c

3c

waistline edge

right garment front   left garment front

5c. Cut a piece of ¾-inch-wide elastic ½ inch longer than your waistline measurement.

6c. Lap the ends of the elastic ½ inch and join them by machine stitching a small rectangle.

7c. Insert a pin about 1 inch from the join. Then insert three more pins to divide the elastic into four equal parts.

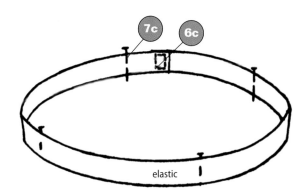

elastic

Basic Elastic Waistband
Basic waistband with alternate casing

8c. Place the elastic inside the garment, lining up the inner edge along the casing fold-line markings. Match and pin at the pin markers.

9c. Stretching the elastic as you sew, attach the elastic to the garment by running a line of machine zigzag stitching just inside the inner edge of the elastic. As you reach a pin, remove it.

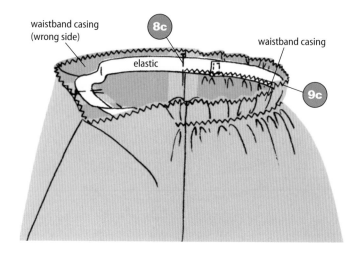

waistband casing (wrong side)

elastic

8c

waistband casing

9c

10c. Fold the waistband casing to the inside of the garment along the inner edge of the elastic. Pin at the center front, center back and the sides.

11c. Sewing from the wrong side of the garment and stretching the elasticized casing as you sew, run a line of machine zigzag stitching ¼ inch from the unattached edge of the casing. Use the outer edge of the presser foot lined up with the edge of the casing as a guide. Remove each pin as you reach it.

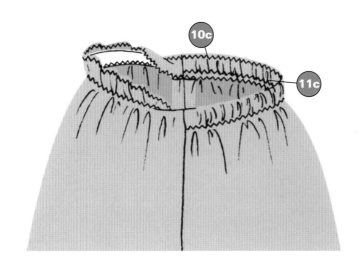

Basic Elastic Waistband
Basic waistband with no casing

1d. Cut the garment sections following your pattern instructions with the following exception: leave only a ¼-inch seam allowance above the casing fold line or waist seam line. Then assemble the garment, stitching all seams closed up to the waistline edge. Press open the seams.

2d. Turn the garment right side out.

3d. Fold the waistline edge of the garment to the wrong side ¼ inch and press.

4d. Insert a pin along the folded top edge of the garment at a seam. Pin from the wrong side of the garment. Then insert three additional pins along the folded edge, dividing the waistline into four equal parts.

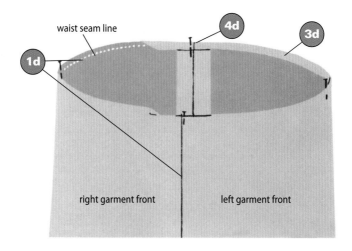

waist seam line

right garment front   left garment front

5d. Prepare a piece of ½- or ¾-inch-wide elastic for the waistband as shown in Steps 5c–7c *(page 17)*.

6d. Place the elastic inside the garment, lining up the outer edge of the elastic just below the folded waistline edge of the garment. Match and pin at the pin markers, using one set of pins for pinning and removing the other set.

7d. Sewing from the wrong side of the garment and stretching the elastic as you sew, run a line of machine zigzag stitching just inside the outer edge of the elastic. As you reach each pin, remove it.

8d. Make a second line of zigzag stitching close to the inner edge of the elastic.

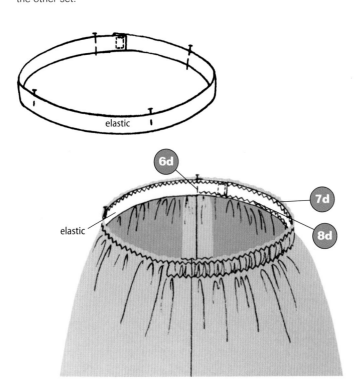

Drawstring Waist
Making the drawstring opening

1. To provide a finished opening for the drawstring, mark the position for two vertical buttonholes as indicated on the pattern, whether for a skirt, as shown in this example, or for a dress or tunic. Then make a machine or hand buttonhole *(page 160-161)* or follow the instructions that are provided with your sewing machine.

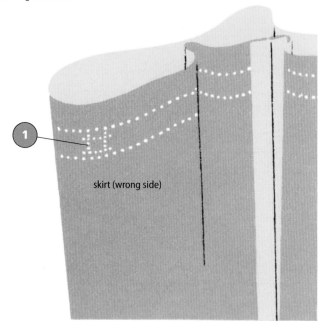

skirt (wrong side)

Preparing the casing

2. Make the casing following the instructions for a Basic Elastic Waistband pages 10–11.

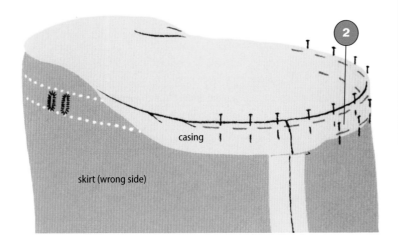

casing

skirt (wrong side)

Drawstring Waist
Making the drawstring

3. For the drawstring cut out a strip of fabric on the grain—that is, parallel to the lengthwise, or selvage, edge. The strip should be twice the width of the casing between the two parallel rows of stitching plus ¼ inch; the length of the strip should be 1½ times the circumference of your waist.

4. Fold over the two lengthwise edges ¼ inch toward the wrong side. Pin at 1-inch intervals. Baste and remove the pins.

5. Fold the strip in half lengthwise with the folded edges inside and pin the folded edges together at 1-inch intervals. Baste and remove the pins.

6. Machine stitch on the right side, the side that will be visible in the finished drawstring, as close to the folded edges as possible.

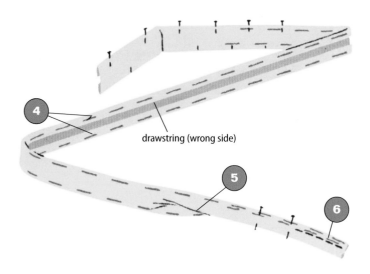

drawstring (wrong side)

Finishing the drawstring casing and ends of drawstring

7. Pull the drawstring through the casing by attaching a safety pin to one end and inserting it into one of the buttonholes. Then push the drawstring through the casing until the safety pin end comes out of the other buttonhole.

8. Tie a tight knot as close to each end of the drawstring as possible.

9. Trim off any material extending beyond the knot with a sharp scissors.

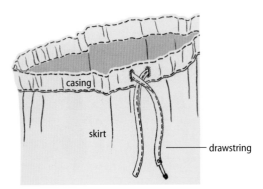

casing

skirt

drawstring

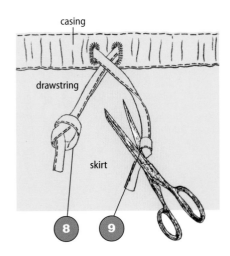

casing

drawstring

skirt

Lapped Zipper

Preparing the side seam for the insertion of the zipper

1. If your pattern does not provide an extra-wide seam allowance of 1 inch for the side zipper, add it to the side seam as you cut out the fabric.

2. With wrong sides facing out, pin closed the left side seam (*white*), then mark (*green*) the length of the zipper: Place the open zipper face down on the center back seam line so that the

zipper's top stop is ¼ inch below the markings for the neck seam line. Mark the position of the top and bottom stops of the zipper on the center back seam line with chalk or a pin. Then re-mark, using a basting stitch (*page 164*) as indicated in green; extend these marks across the two center back seam allowances.

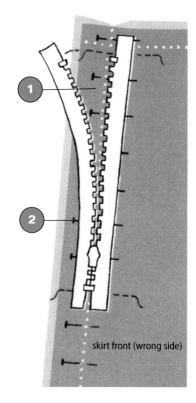

skirt front (wrong side)

3. Baste *(red)* the side seam from the hemline up to the marking for the bottom stop; remove the pins. Machine stitch *(blue)*, then remove the basting.

4. Baste closed the remainder of the side seam directly on the seam-line marking from the bottom stop to the waistline edge.

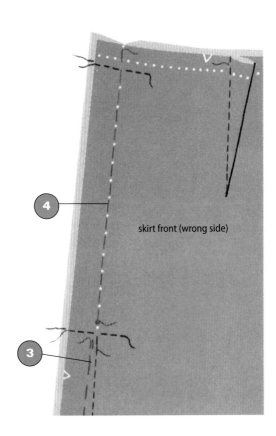

skirt front (wrong side)

Lapped Zipper
Sewing the zipper to the skirt back

5. Press open the side seam.

6. Lay the garment down on the back section and extend the back seam allowance so that it lies flat.

7. Place the open zipper face down on the extended back seam allowance, with its top and bottom stops at the horizontal markings made in Step 2.

The teeth should be flush against the closed side seam. Pin the left tape to the back seam allowance.

8. Baste the zipper tape to the extended back seam allowance close to the teeth. Work from the bottom of the zipper tape to the top, machine basting with a zipper foot or using short hand stitches. Remove the pins.

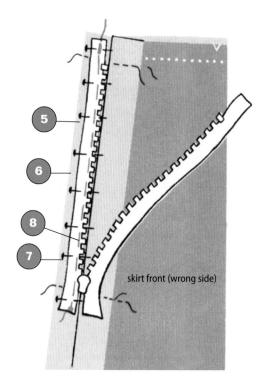

skirt front (wrong side)

9. Close the zipper and fold the back seam allowance under the garment along the line of basting made in Step 8, thus causing the zipper to flip up.

10. Pin together all layers of the fabric—the front seam allowance, the skirt front and back, and the back seam allowance.

11. Using a zipper foot, machine stitch along the narrow strip of folded seam allowance from the bottom of the zipper tape to the top. Remove the pins.

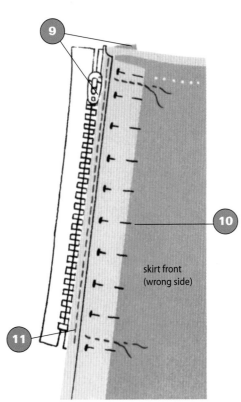

skirt front
(wrong side)

Lapped Zipper
Sewing the zipper to the skirt front

12. Turn the skirt right side out.

13. Hold the zipper inside the skirt so that it lies flat on the seam. Pin it in place across both seam allowances.

14. Hand baste ½ inch from the side seam up the skirt front from the bottom stop marking to the top edge, sewing through all layers—the skirt front, front seam allowance and the zipper tape. Remove pins.

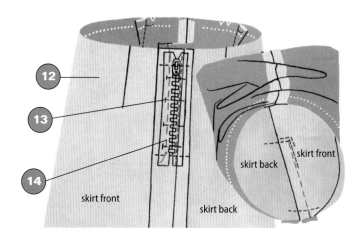

skirt front

skirt back

skirt front

skirt back

15. Turn the skirt wrong side out.

16. Slide the skirt front, wrong side down, under the zipper foot. Beginning at the side seam and following a line ⅛ inch outside the marking for the

bottom stop made in Step 2, page 110, stitch across the bottom and up the length of the zipper to the top edge of the garment. Then snip open the side seam basting, remove all other bastings and press.

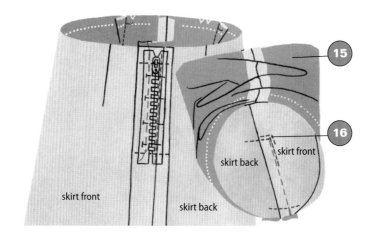

skirt front

skirt back

skirt front

skirt back

Women's Fly-Front Zipper
Preparing the pants front

1. If your pattern does not include fly facings as part of the front sections, pin the fly pattern to the front section when laying the pattern on the fabric. Cut as if one piece.

2. Baste *(green)* along the center front seam-line marking *(white)* of the left front section, stitching the length of the fly facing.

3. Run a line of basting parallel to the basted line made in Step 2, and ¼ inch toward the fly facing. This will become the fly fold line.

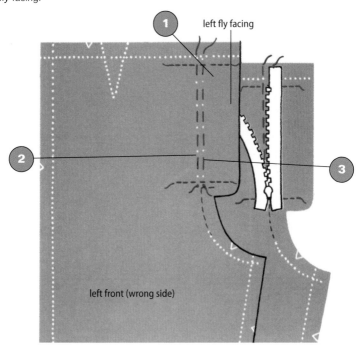

left fly facing

left front (wrong side)

4. Place the open zipper face down on the left center seam line, so that the zipper's top stop is ¼ inch below the waist seam line.

5. Mark the position of the top and bottom stops with chalk or pins; re-mark with a basting stitch (*page 164*).

6. To reinforce the crotch, machine stitch (*blue*) a line beginning at the left fly fold line ¼ inch below the marking for the bottom stop. Stitch across from the fold line to the center seam line and then down 1 inch along the center seam line.

7. Repeat Steps 2–6 on the right front pants section.

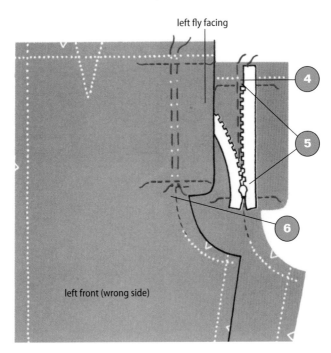

left fly facing

left front (wrong side)

Women's Fly-Front Zipper
Assembling the pants

8. To ensure the proper hang of the garment, assemble the pants in the following sequence: sew and press the darts, the outer leg seams and the inner leg seams. Then join the legs by sewing the center seam, beginning at the center back waistline and ending at the bottom stop marking on the center front seam line.

9. With the tips of a scissors, clip into the center front seam allowance at the base of the fly facing, cutting diagonally to within 1/16 inch of the line of reinforcement stitching made in Step 6.

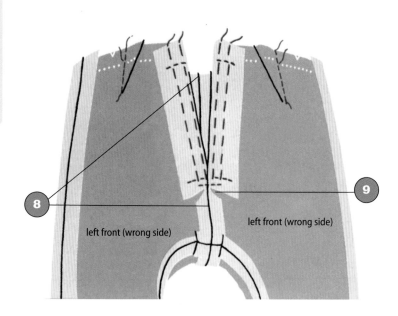

left front (wrong side)

left front (wrong side)

Sewing the zipper to the right fly facing

10. Place the right front of the pants wrong side down and extend the right fly facing so that it lies flat.

11. Place the open zipper face down on the extended right fly facing, so that the top stop is on the horizontal marking made in Step 5. The teeth should be flush against the basted fold line. Pin the right zipper tape to the facing.

12. Baste *(red)* the zipper tape to the right fly facing ¼ inch from the outer edge of the tape. Remove the pins.

13. Using a zipper foot, machine stitch ⅛ inch from the teeth. Remove the basting.

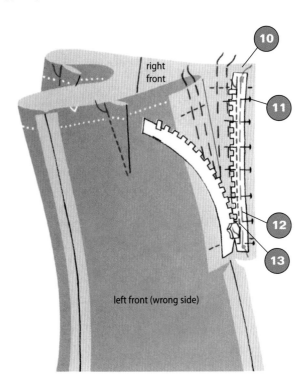

right
front

left front (wrong side)

Women's Fly-Front Zipper
Sewing the zipper to the left front

14. Turn the pants right side out.

15. Fold the left fly facing to the inside along the basted fold line.

16. Pin and baste the loose, unstitched zipper tape, wrong side down, to the left front through all layers—the pants front, fly facing and zipper tape—with the top stop of the zipper at the horizontal marking and the zipper teeth extending just beyond the fold of the fabric. Remove the pins.

17. On the side of the fabric that will be visible in the completed garment, machine stitch the zipper to the left front near the fold. Close the zipper.

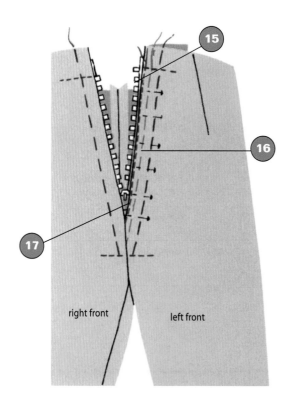

right front   left front

Finishing the fly front

18. Lap the right front over the zipper until the fabric lies flat, covers the teeth and meets the center seam line of the left front. Pin in place close to the folded edge.

19. Hand baste the zipper from top to bottom on the right front, staying 1 inch from the folded edge. Baste to within 1 inch of the bottom stop, then curve the basting until it meets the center seam. Remove the pins.

20. Turn the pants wrong side out.

21. Slide the pants wrong side down under the zipper foot and begin stitching at the center seam, just outside the basting. To reinforce the fly, stitch forward two stitches, then back two stitches and then forward the length of the zipper. Remove basting and press.

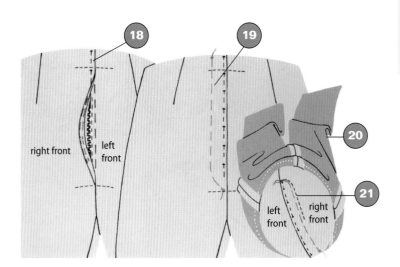

right front   left front

left front   right front

Men's Fly-Front Zipper
Preparing the pants front

1. If you have not already done so, run a line of basting *(green)* along the waist seam-line marking *(white)* of each front section so that it will show on both sides of the fabric.

2. On the right pants front, run a line of basting parallel to the center seam line and ¼ inch outside it, extending from the waistline edge to the bottom of the fly opening marked on the pattern; this will become the fly fold line.

3. To reinforce the crotch on each front section, machine stitch *(blue)* along the center seam line, beginning 1 inch below the marking for the bottom of the fly opening and ending 1 inch above that point.

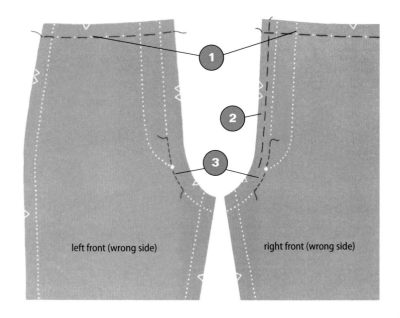

left front (wrong side)

right front (wrong side)

Joining the pants front

4. Pin together the pants front pieces along the center seam line.

5. Baste *(red)* along the center seam line at the crotch, then remove the pins. Machine stitch from the mark for the bottom of the fly opening to 1 inch from the inner leg seam line.

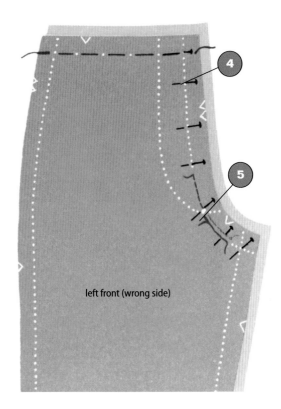

left front (wrong side)

Men's Fly-Front Zipper
Making the left fly

6. Pin and baste the interfacing (*dark gray*) to the wrong side of the left fly. Remove the pins, machine stitch, then remove the basting.

7. Trim the seam allowance—of the interfacing only—close to the machine stitching.

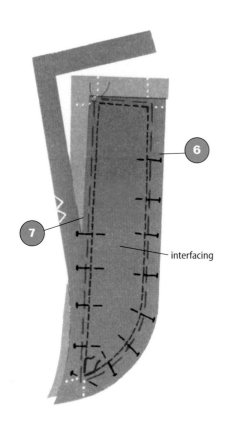

interfacing

Attaching the left fly to the left pants front

8. With the wrong sides of the fabric facing outward, pin the left fly to the left pants front along the center seam line, making sure that the markings for the seam intersections and notches match.

9. Baste the left fly to the left pants front along the center seam line, starting at the top edge of the pants and ending at the bottom of the fly opening. Remove the pins, machine stitch and remove the bastings.

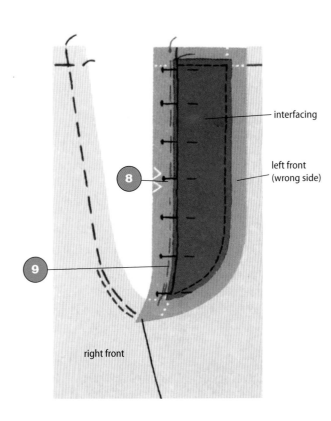

interfacing

left front
(wrong side)

right front

Men's Fly-Front Zipper
Attaching the left fly to the left pants front

10. Fold the right pants front over the left pants front.

11. Clip through the center seam allowances at the base of the fly, pushing away the fly fabric itself so that it is not clipped.

12. Trim the center seam allowance of the fly to within ⅛ inch of the machine stitching, from the diagonal clip made in Step 11 to the waistline edge.

13. Trim the center seam allowance of the left pants front to within ¼ inch of the machine stitching, from the diagonal clip to the waistline edge.

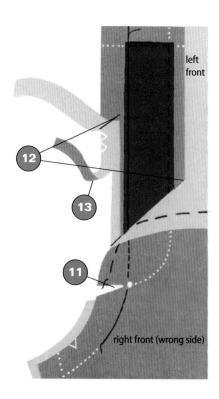

left front

right front (wrong side)

Attaching the zipper to the left fly

14. Press the center seam toward the fly, then place the garment on its left front and extend the fly.

15. Place the closed zipper face down on the left fly, with the bottom stop ¼ inch above the bottom of the seam opening, and the right edge of the tape on the pressed seam fold. Pin the left tape to the fly. If the tape extends above the top edge of the pants, cut it off according to the directions given on the zipper package.

16. Baste the zipper tape to the left fly ¼ inch from the teeth. Remove the pins.

17. Using a zipper foot, attach the zipper to the left fly with two rows of machine stitching, one row along the left edge of the basted tape and a second row close to the teeth.

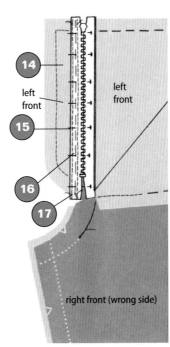

left front

left front

right front (wrong side)

Men's Fly-Front Zipper
Finishing the left fly front

18. With the pants wrong side down, fold under the left fly, causing the zipper to flip up. Pin the fly to the left front fabric at 1-inch intervals so that it lies flat.

19. Hand baste the left fly to the left front in a line 1½ inches from the folded edge. When you come to within 1½ inches of the bottom of the fly opening, curve the basting in to meet the center seam at the bottom of the opening. Do not catch the unstitched bottom end of the zipper tape in the stitches. Remove the pins.

20. Machine stitch the left fly to the left front, starting at the bottom curve just outside the basting. To reinforce the fly front, stitch forward two stitches, then back two stitches, and then forward to the waist. Remove all basting.

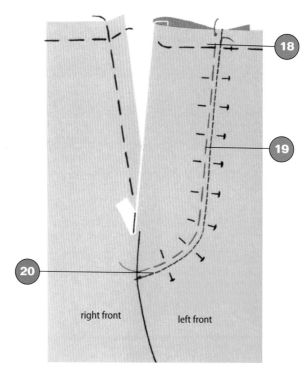

right front

left front

Basting the zipper to the right front

21. Fold under the seam allowance of the right front along the basted fold line and press.

22. Place the folded edge of the right pants front over the zipper tape and pin at the top edges, making sure that the markings for the waist seam lines on both sections of the pants are aligned and that the zipper teeth extend just beyond the edge of the fold.

23. Opening the zipper as you proceed, pin the folded edge of the pants to the zipper tape close to the teeth.

24. Baste ¼ inch from the folded edge and remove the pins.

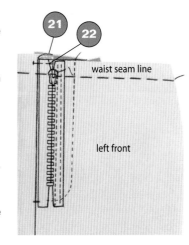

waist seam line

left front

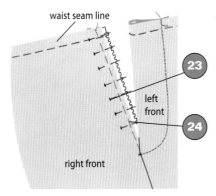

waist seam line

left front

right front

Men's Fly-Front Zipper
Making the right fly

25. With the wrong sides of the fabric facing outward, pin the two pieces of the right fly together along the long curved, unnotched edge.

26. Baste, remove the pins, and then machine stitch along the curved edge. Remove the bastings.

27. Trim the seam allowance of the stitched curved edge to ¼ inch.

28. Notch the curve of the trimmed seam allowance.

29. Turn the fly right side out and press the stitched seam flat. Topstitch with a line of machine stitching ⅛ inch from the sewn curved edge.

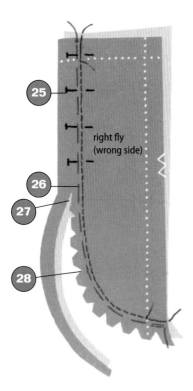

right fly
(wrong side)

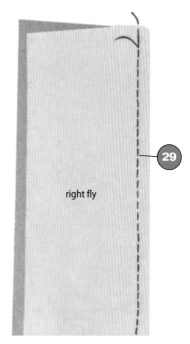

right fly

Attaching the right fly to the right pants front

30. Lay the right pants front wrong side down over the right fly, setting the teeth ⅝ inch from the unstitched notched edge of the fly; pin to hold in place.

31. Baste from the bottom of the fly opening to the top, close to the folded edge. Remove the pins. Using a zipper foot, machine stitch, reinforcing the fly by stitching forward two stitches, then back two stitches and then forward the length of the zipper. Remove all bastings and press.

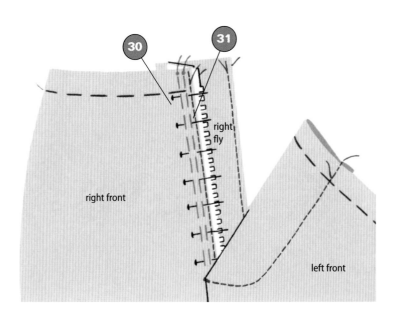

right fly

right front

left front

Trouser Waistband
Preparing the interfacing

1. If the waistband and Interfacing *(dark gray)* are cut from the same pattern piece, fold the interfacing in half lengthwise and mark a center fold line with chalk.

2a. Cutting ¼ inch above the center fold line, trim away the long part of the interfacing that has no pattern notches.

2b. If the interfacing has not been cut from the same pattern piece, make sure that it is the same length and ¼ inch more than half the width of the waistband.

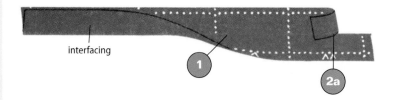

interfacing

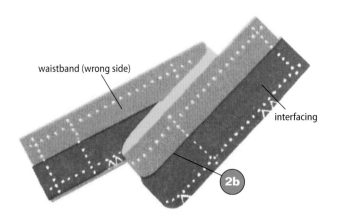

waistband (wrong side)

interfacing

Attaching the interfacing

3. Place the interfacing on the wrong side of the waistband, lining it up with the notched edge. Pin together, matching the notches and pattern markings *(white)*.

4. Baste *(red)* the interfacing to the waistband along the notched side and both ends. Remove the pins.

5. Hand stitch *(black)* the interfacing to the waistband ⅛ inch above the center fold line, using thread the same color as the fabric. Make ½-inch stitches on the interfacing side but do not stitch through the waistband material; pick up only a thread of the waistband fabric.

6. Trim the interfacing close to the bastings along the three outer edges. Do not trim along the center fold line.

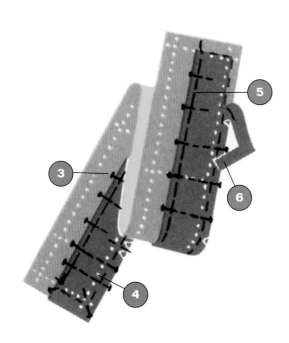

Trouser Waistband
Sewing the waistband

7. Fold the waistband in half lengthwise, wrong side out.

8. Pin along the seam markings around the corner of the waistband, from the lap line to the folded edge. Then baste and remove the pins.

9. Machine stitch *(blue)* along the seam markings, from the lap line around the corner to the folded edge.

10. Pin the other end of the waistband together. Then baste along the end seam markings and remove the pins.

11. Machine stitch along the end seam markings, beginning at the corner where the end and long seam markings intersect—not at the edge of the fabric.

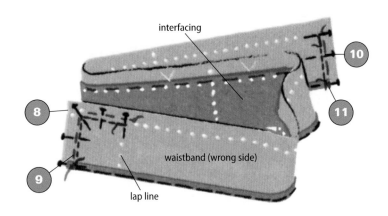

interfacing

waistband (wrong side)

lap line

12. Clip into the seam allowance diagonally at the lap line, cutting close to but not into the stitching.

13. At the lapped end, trim the seam allowance to ¼ inch and trim both corners diagonally.

14. Trim the seam allowance at the other end of the waistband to ¼ inch and trim diagonally at the folded edge.

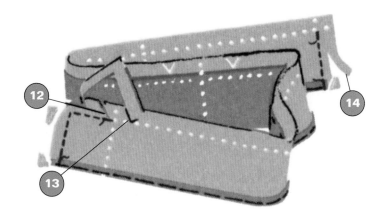

Trouser Waistband
Sewing the waistband to the garment

15. Turn the waistband and the garment right sides out.

16. Pin the long notched edge of the waistband to the garment along the waist seam-line markings, matching notches and seams. Be sure the sides of the waistband and garment fabric that will be visible in the finished garment are facing each other.

17. Baste along the waist seam-line markings. Remove the pins, and then machine stitch.

18. Trim the garment seam allowance to ⅛ inch. Trim the waistband seam allowance to ¼ inch. Trim the seam allowance of the long unstitched waistband edge to ¼ inch.

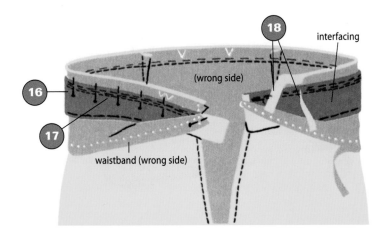

interfacing

(wrong side)

waistband (wrong side)

The final touches

19. Turn over the long unstitched edge of the waistband to the inside of the garment.

20. Fold under the unstitched edge along the seam marking and pin it to the garment, then baste and remove the pins.

21. Hand stitch the folded edge of the waistband to the garment with a slip stitch *(page 169)*. Do not stitch into the garment fabric but pick up only a few threads of the seam allowance. Remove all bastings and press.

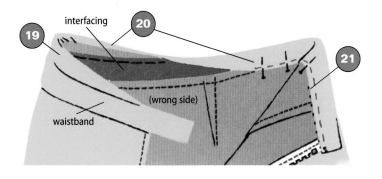

interfacing

(wrong side)

waistband

Waist with Ribbon Facing
Preparing the ribbon and the skirt or pants

1. Measure the waistline of the skirt or pants and cut a piece of grosgrain ribbon 6 inches longer than the waistline.

2. Measure in 3½ inches from one end of the ribbon, and make a dart in the ribbon ⅛ inch deep at the top. Make identical darts at 3-inch intervals along the length of the ribbon.

3. Press all the darts in one direction.

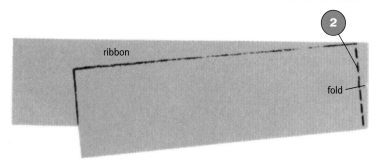

ribbon

2

fold

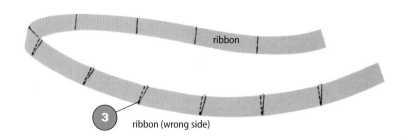

ribbon

3

ribbon (wrong side)

Attaching the ribbon

4. With the garment right side out and the ribbon wrong side down, align the inner edge of the ribbon with the waistband stitching line on the garment. Start the end of the ribbon ½ inch beyond the zipper opening edge.

5. Pin the ribbon around the waistline. At the other end, trim the ribbon to extend ½ inch beyond the zipper.

6. Baste the ribbon to the garment close to the inner edge of the ribbon. Remove the pins.

7. Machine stitch as close as possible to the inner edge of the ribbon. Remove the basting.

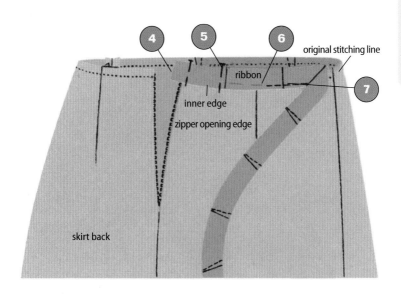

original stitching line

ribbon

inner edge

zipper opening edge

skirt back

Waist with Ribbon Facing
Finishing the waistline

8. Turn the garment wrong side out. Fold the waistline down so that the fold lies ⅛ inch above the inner edge of the ribbon. Press.

9. Unfold the waistline. Fold one end of the ribbon over the zipper opening edge so the fold tapers, as shown.

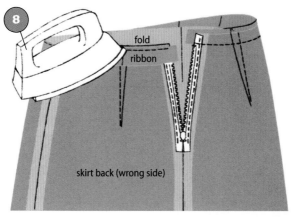

fold

ribbon

skirt back (wrong side)

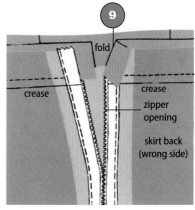

fold

crease

crease

zipper opening

skirt back (wrong side)

10. Refold the ribbon along the crease pressed in Step 8.

11. Pin the folded end of the ribbon to the zipper tape.

12. Hem the ribbon to the zipper tape. Remove the pin. Repeat Steps 9–11 on the other end of the ribbon.

13. Using a hemming stitch (page 167), attach the ribbon to the seam allowances and darts of the garment.

14. Sew a hook to one side of the zipper opening and an eye to the other side so that each extends slightly beyond the folded edge of the grosgrain ribbon.

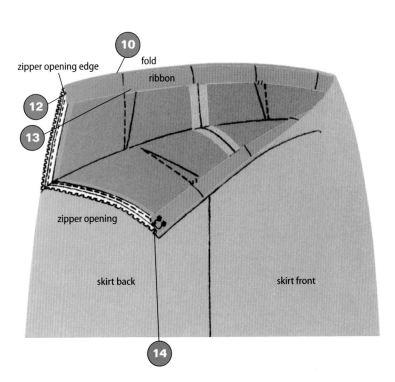

zipper opening edge

fold

ribbon

zipper opening

skirt back

skirt front

Select-n-Stitch Dress Waists

The best dresses combine a fitted top and body-skimming bottom into a pretty, pleasing whole. Simple techniques ensure the pieces join smoothly and hang straight.

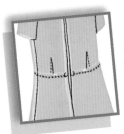

Basic Seamed Waistline,
page 60

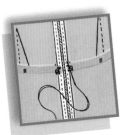

Ribbon-Reinforced Seamed
Waistline, page 64

Inset Waistband,
page 68

Single-Elasticized Waist,
page 74

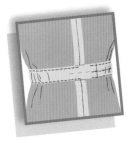

Double-Elasticized Waist,
page 78

Peplum,
page 80

Basic Seamed Waistline
Preparing the pieces

1. With the completed skirt turned wrong side out, run a line of machine stitching along the waist seam line to prevent the curved edge from stretching out of shape.

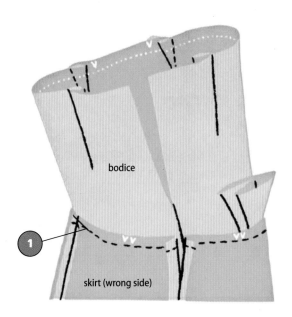

bodice

skirt (wrong side)

2. With the bodice turned right side out, insert it upside down into the skirt. The right sides of both pieces—the sides that will be visible in the finished garment—will then face together.

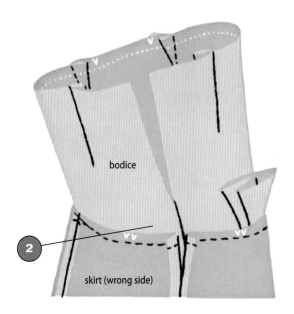

bodice

2

skirt (wrong side)

Basic Seamed Waistline
Attaching the skirt and bodice

3. Pin the skirt to the bodice at the waistline, matching side seams and notches as well as center front and center back.

4. Baste the skirt and bodice together along the waist seam line. Remove the pins.

5. Machine stitch around the waist along the seam line. Remove the basting.

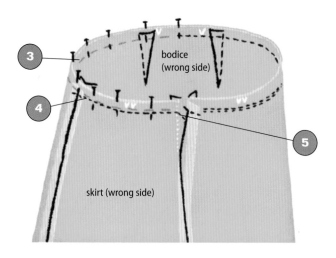

bodice
(wrong side)

skirt (wrong side)

Finishing the waist

6. Pull out the bodice from inside the skirt and press the seam allowances upward toward the bodice.

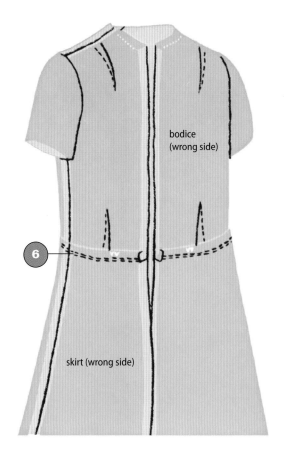

bodice
(wrong side)

6

skirt (wrong side)

Ribbon-Reinforced Seamed Waistline

Preparing the garment

1. Join the bodice and skirt, following the instructions for the basic seamed waistline (page 60-63). Finish the closure with a zipper or buttons.

2. Close the zipper or buttons. Then turn the garment wrong side out.

3. Measure the circumference of the waist seam line, including the zipper or button closure facing.

SELECT-N-STITCH DRESS WAISTS

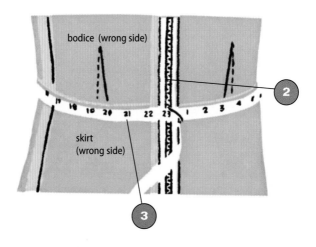

bodice (wrong side)

skirt
(wrong side)

Alligning the ribbon

4. Cut ⅝-inch-wide grosgrain ribbon 1½ inches longer than the waistline circumference as measured in Step 3.

5. Fold ¾ inch of the ribbon under at one end and pin the folded end to the waist seam line allowance of the garment, centering the ribbon on the seam line and aligning the folded end with the center of the closure.

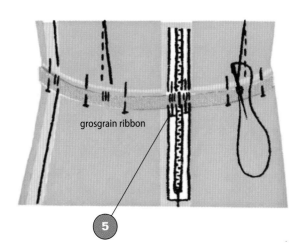

grosgrain ribbon

5

Ribbon-Reinforced Seamed Waistline
Attaching the ribbon

6. Fasten the remaining ribbon around the waistline along the seam, inserting pins at 2-inch intervals. Fold the loose end of the ribbon under at the center of the closure. Pin so that the two folded ends meet exactly.

7. Using thread knotted at the end, stitch the ribbon to the waistline seam allowance just above the waist seam line by making three or four ¼-inch-long overlapping stitches at each of the side seams and darts, at both edges of the zipper tape or closure facing, and finally at the center of the section of the garment directly opposite the closure. Remove the pins.

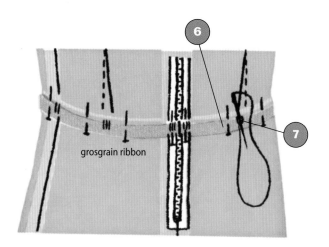

grosgrain ribbon

Finishing the waist

8. Turn back one ribbon end and place a hook as shown on the underside ⅛ inch from the folded end. Using a double strand of thread knotted at the end, stitch the hook to the ribbon by making three or four ¼-inch-long overlapping stitches at the end of each metal ring and at the bend of the hook. Be sure to sew through both layers of the ribbon to hold the fold in place. Secure the end of the thread with a fastening stitch (page 166).

9. Lift up the opposite ribbon end and place an eye on the underside so that the rim of the eye protrudes just beyond the folded edge. Stitch the eye in place in the same way that you stitched the hook. The folded ribbon edges should meet exactly when hook and eye are fastened.

10. Try on the garment and if the ribbon pulls the waistline out of shape, clip out the fastening stitches made in Step 7. Re-pin the ribbon to the waistline as shown in Step 6 and sew in new fastening stitches.

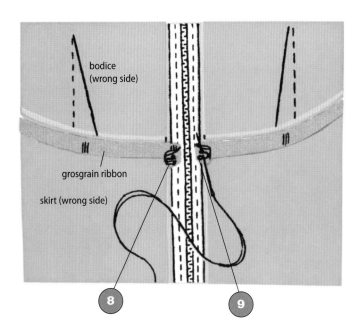

bodice
(wrong side)

grosgrain ribbon

skirt (wrong side)

8

9

Inset Waistband
Preparing the waistband

1. Cut an interfacing for the waistband from special interfacing fabric, using the pattern piece for the inset waistband, and transfer the pattern markings to the interfacing.

2. Pin the interfacing to the wrong side of the waistband, matching all pattern markings.

3. Baste the interfacing and waistband together along the seam lines. Remove the pins.

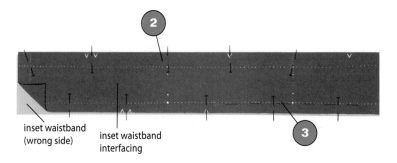

inset waistband (wrong side)

inset waistband interfacing

Attaching the waistband to the bodice

4. With the bodice of the dress turned right side out, place the waistband over it, interfaced side up. Align the bottom edge of the bodice with the edge of the waistband that has matching pattern markings. Pin at the bottom edge.

5. Baste the bodice and waistband together along the seam line at the pinned edge. Remove the pins.

6. Fold down the waistband.

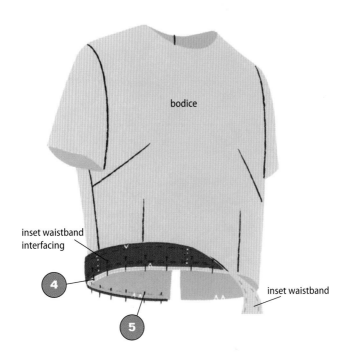

bodice

inset waistband interfacing

inset waistband

Inset Waistband
Attaching the waistband to the skirt

7. With the completed skirt of the dress turned wrong side out, run a line of machine stitching along the, waist seam line to prevent the curved edge from stretching out of shape.

8. With the bodice turned right side out, insert it upside down into the skirt. The right sides of both pieces—the sides that will be visible in the finished garment—will then face together.

9. Pin the unattached edge of the waistband to the waistline seam allowance of the skirt, matching all pattern markings and keeping together the sides of the fabric that will be visible in the finished garment.

10. Baste along the waist seam line of the pinned edge of the skirt. Remove the pins.

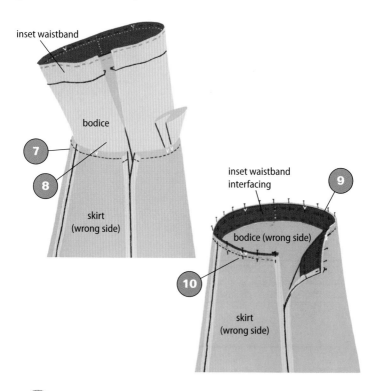

inset waistband

bodice

7

8

skirt
(wrong side)

inset waistband
interfacing

9

bodice (wrong side)

10

skirt
(wrong side)

Finishing the waistband

11. Pull out the bodice from inside the skirt and with the garment wrong side out, machine stitch the waistband first to the bodice and then to the skirt along the bastings made in Steps 5 and 10. Remove all bastings.

12. To reduce bulkiness, trim and grade the seam allowances at the top and bottom of the waistband—that is, trim the interfacing seam allowance to ⅛ inch, the waistband seam allowance to ¼ inch, and the bodice and skirt seam allowances to ½ inch.

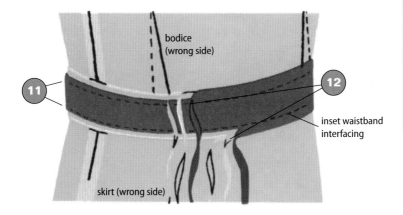

bodice
(wrong side)

11

12

inset waistband
interfacing

skirt (wrong side)

Inset Waistband
Finishing the waistband

13. Press the seam allowances from the bodice waist seam line down to the waistband, and from the skirt waist seam line up to the waistband.

14. Using the pattern pieces for the inset waistband, cut out a lining for the waistband from lining fabric. Transfer the pattern markings to the wrong side of the lining.

15. Pin the lining to the garment, wrong sides together, matching all pattern markings and aligning the top and bottom seam lines of the lining with the waist seam lines of the bodice and skirt.

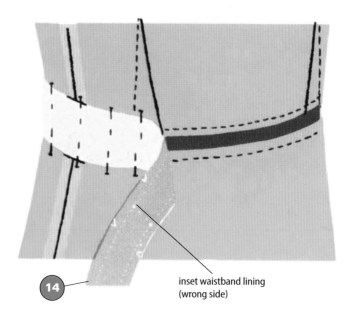

14

inset waistband lining
(wrong side)

16. Remove one of the pins holding the lining to the bodice, and fold under the top edge of the lining so that it just covers the waist seam line of the bodice, then replace the pin. Repeat—removing, folding and replacing one pin at a time—all around the top edge of the waistband.

17. Repeat this process around the bottom edge of the waistband so that the folded edge of the bottom of the lining just covers the waist seam line of the skirt.

18. Slip stitch *(page 169)* the lining to the garment along the machine stitching made in Step 11. Remove the pins and press lightly.

19. Insert the zipper or finish the button closure, then fold under the ends of the lining and slip stitch the folded edges to the zipper tape or closure facing.

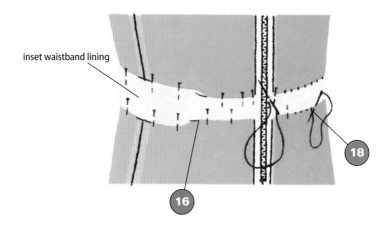

inset waistband lining

Single-Elasticized Waist
Seaming the casing strip

1. Cut out the strip of fabric that will form the casing, or tunnel, for the elasticized waist, using the pattern piece provided or the measurements given in the pattern instruction guide.

2. With the wrong sides facing out, pin and baste the ends together. Remove the pins.

3. Join the ends with a line of machine stitching ⅝ inch in from the edge. Remove the basting, and press the seam open.

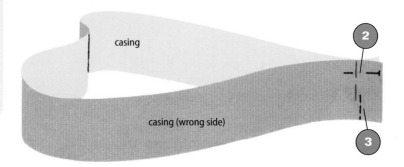

casing

casing (wrong side)

Preparing the edges of the casing strip

4. With the wrong side facing in, fold the top edge of the casing over ¼ inch toward the wrong side. Pin at 1-inch intervals and baste. Remove the pins.

5. Fold, pin and baste the bottom edge of the casing in the same way. Remove the pins.

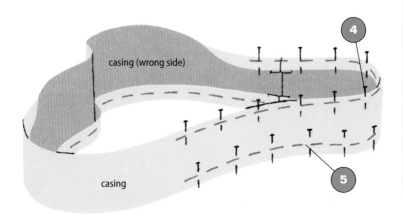

casing (wrong side)

casing

Single-Elasticized Waist
Basting the casing strip inside the garment

6. Turn the garment wrong side out. Make sure the waistline pattern markings have been transferred to the garment.

7. Turn the casing right side out and slip it over the garment. The wrong side of the garment and the wrong side of the casing will be facing each other.

8. Pin both edges of the casing to the garment at 1-inch intervals following the pattern markings on the garment.

9. Baste the casing to the garment along both edges. Leave an open space at the bottom edge wide enough to insert the elastic. Remove the pins.

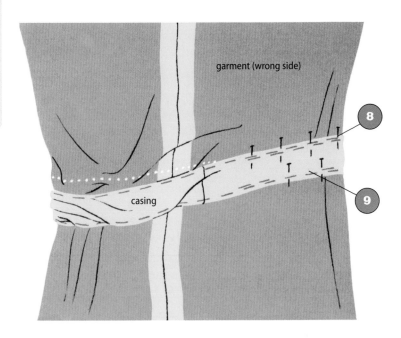

garment (wrong side)

casing

Finishing the casing

10. Machine stitch both edges of the casing to the garment ⅛ inch in from the edge, leaving open the space along the bottom edge where the elastic will be inserted.

11. Cut a length of elastic 1 inch longer than your waistline measurement (to allow for joining the ends). Attach a safety pin to one end. Push the pinned end of the elastic into the space left open in the lower edge of the casing and thread it through the casing.

12. After the elastic has been pulled through the casing, remove the safety pin, overlap the ends by 1 inch and join them with three evenly spaced parallel rows of machine stitching (for extra strength).

13. Pull on the casing so the ends of the elastic disappear into the casing. Close the opening through which elastic was inserted, using a slip stitch (*page 169*). Turn the garment right side out.

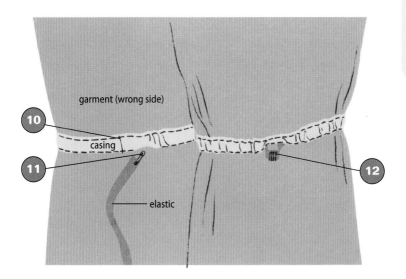

garment (wrong side)

10

casing

11

elastic

12

Double-Elasticized Waist
Preparing the casing strip

1. Cut out the strip of fabric that will form the casing, or tunnel, for the double-elasticized waist, using the pattern piece provided or the measurements given in the pattern instruction guide. The fabric will be twice the depth required for the single casing.

2. Make the wider casing following the instructions for the narrower, single-elasticized waist, pages 74-76, Steps 2–9.

3. Machine stitch both edges of the casing to the garment ⅛ inch in from the edge, leaving an open space at the bottom of the casing to insert the elastic for the bottom half.

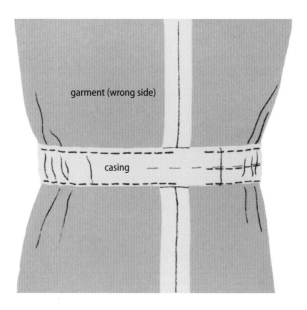

garment (wrong side)

casing

Finishing the casing

4. Baste and machine stitch another line halfway between the top and bottom edges to form the double casing, leaving an open space to insert the elastic for the top half of the casing. Remove the bastings.

5. Finish the double-elasticized casing following the instructions for the single elasticized casing, page 77, Steps 11–13.

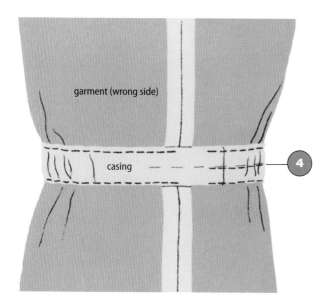

garment (wrong side)

casing

4

Peplum
Preparing the garment

1. Run a line of basting stitches along the pattern markings for the waistline seam, the center front line and the center back seam on both the skirt and bodice so that the lines will be visible on both sides of the fabric.

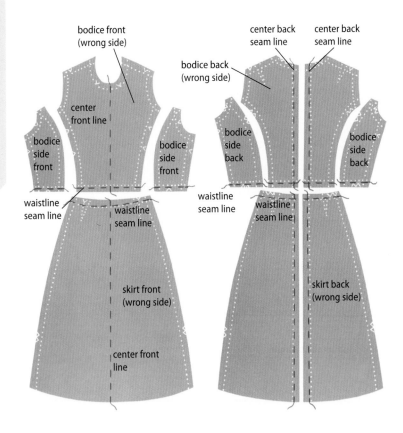

bodice front
(wrong side)

center back
seam line

center back
seam line

bodice back
(wrong side)

center
front line

bodice
side
front

bodice
side
front

bodice
side
back

bodice
side
back

waistline
seam line

waistline
seam line

waistline
seam line

waistline
seam line

skirt front
(wrong side)

skirt back
(wrong side)

center front
line

2. Baste the bodice pieces together, then baste the skirt pieces together. Try the bodice and skirt on separately and adjust for fit. Stitch and press all darts and seams except the waistline seam.

3. To determine that the waistline will fall in the right place, baste the bodice to the skirt along the waistline seam markings and try the dress on. If you need to make adjustments at the waistline, remove the old bastings and run a new line of basting stitches on both the bodice and the skirt to mark the adjustment for the waistline seam. Then separate the bodice from the skirt.

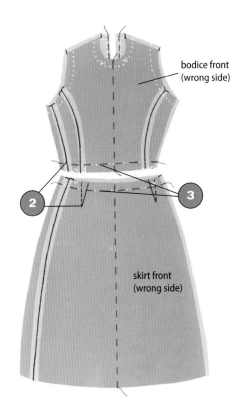

bodice front
(wrong side)

skirt front
(wrong side)

Peplum
Preparing the peplum and the peplum facing

4. If any adjustments were made on the waistline of the skirt in Step 3, draw a new waistline seam marking on the peplum and the facing to correspond, then run a line of basting stitches along the markings for the waistline seam and the center front line on the peplum and the facing so that the lines will be visible on both sides of the fabric.

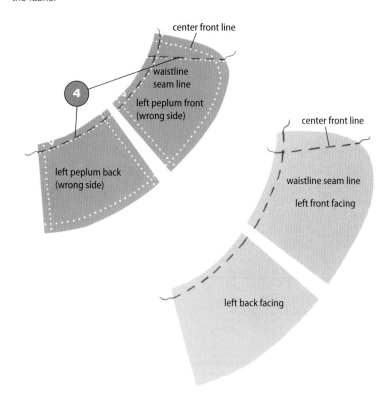

center front line

waistline seam line

left peplum front (wrong side)

left peplum back (wrong side)

center front line

waistline seam line

left front facing

left back facing

Facing the peplum

5. Assemble the left half of the peplum by pinning the left front and left back pieces together along the side seam line.

6. Baste just outside the side seam line and remove the pins.

7. Machine stitch along the seam line and remove the basting.

8. Similarly, pin, baste and machine stitch the left front and left back pieces of the facing for the peplum.

9. Repeat Steps 5–8 to join the right front and right back of the peplum and the peplum facing.

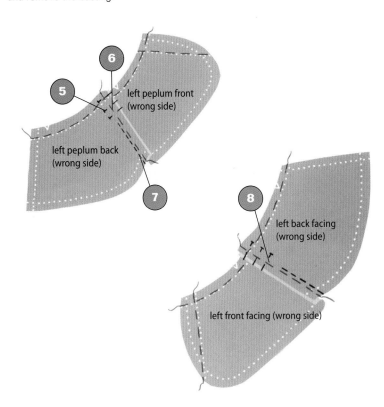

left peplum front (wrong side)

left peplum back (wrong side)

left back facing (wrong side)

left front facing (wrong side)

Peplum
Facing the peplum

10. With the wrong sides out, pin the left facing to the left half of the peplum at both ends and along the long bottom edge. Leave the waistline edge open.

11. Baste the peplum to the facing just outside the seam line. Remove the pins.

12. Machine stitch along the seam line and remove the basting.

13. Trim the seam allowance of the peplum to ¼ inch.

14. Trim the seam allowance of the facing to ⅛ inch.

15. Clip the corners diagonally and clip into the seam allowance along the curved edge, cutting up to but not into the machine stitching.

16. Pin, baste and machine stitch the right facing to the right half of the peplum in the same manner.

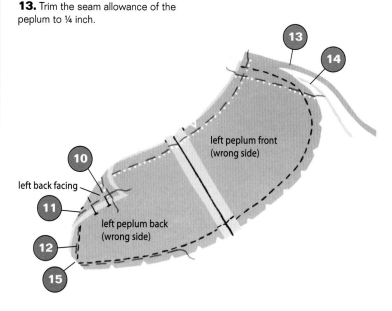

13

14

left peplum front
(wrong side)

10

left back facing

11

left peplum back
(wrong side)

12

15

Finishing the peplum

17. Turn the peplum pieces right side out; push out the corners with the closed end of a blunt pair of scissors.

18. Roll the lower edge of the peplum between your fingers so that the seam joining the peplum to the facing will be turned slightly toward the underside. Baste and press.

19. Baste the open waistline edges of both pieces together just outside the seam-line markings.

20. Run a line of machine stitching just outside the basting to hold the waist seam line in shape. Remove the basting.

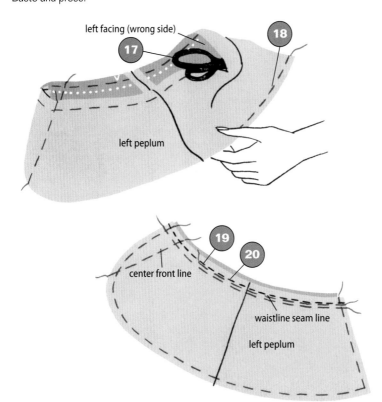

left facing (wrong side)

left peplum

center front line

waistline seam line

left peplum

Peplum
Finishing the peplum

21. Place the two peplum sections on a flat surface, faced sides down. Pin the two sections together so that the right half overlaps the left half and the basted markings indicating the center front lines made in Step 4 are aligned.

22. Baste and remove the pins.

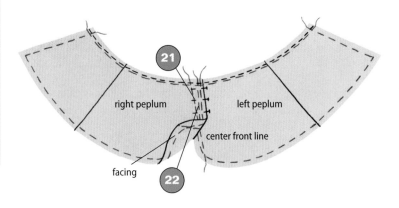

right peplum

left peplum

center front line

facing

Attaching the peplum to the skirt

23. Turn the skirt of the dress right side out.

24. Pin the peplum, faced side down, to the skirt. Pin first at the center front lines, then at the side seams.

25. Align the back edges of the peplum with the seam line markings for the center back seam and pin. Then insert pins around the waist at 1-inch intervals.

26. Baste the peplum to the skirt just outside the waistline seam line and remove the pins.

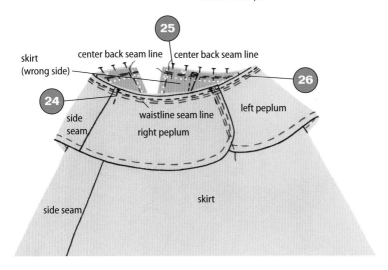

skirt
(wrong side)

center back seam line center back seam line

25

26

24

left peplum

side seam

waistline seam line

right peplum

side seam

skirt

Peplum
Attaching the bodice to the skirt and peplum

27. Turn the skirt and bodice wrong side out. Insert the bodice upside down into the skirt. The right sides of both pieces (the sides that will be visible on completion) should face each other.

28. Pin the bodice to the skirt, matching all pattern markings.

29. Baste just outside the waistline seam line and remove the pins. Remove the bastings made over the tracing wheel markings in Steps 1 and 4.

30. Machine stitch along the seam line and remove the basting.

31. Trim the seam allowance of the bodice to ½ inch.

32. Trim the seam allowances of the peplum to ¼ inch.

33. Trim the seam allowance of the skirt to ½ inch.

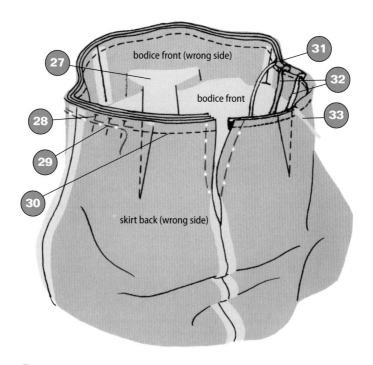

bodice front (wrong side)

bodice front

skirt back (wrong side)

Finishing the dress

34. Turn the garment right side out.

35. Insert a centered zipper in the center back seam, stitching down one edge until you reach the peplum; then take the garment out of the machine, fold up the peplum and resume stitching down to ⅛ inch below the bottom stop of the zipper.

36. Continue stitching across and up the other side of the zipper until you reach the peplum. Again remove the garment from the machine, fold down the peplum this time, and resume stitching up to the neck edge.

37. Remove all bastings and press.

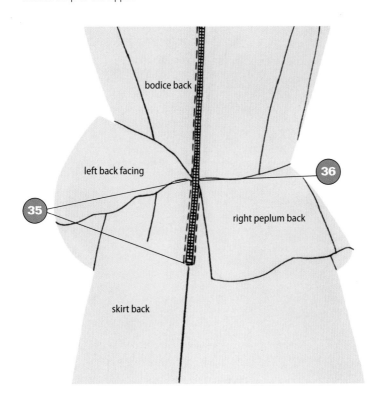

bodice back

left back facing

35

36

right peplum back

skirt back

Select-n-Stitch Waistbands for Jackets

Create a comfortable, flattering fit by applying waistband techniques to athletic or outdoor gear, sweaters, and other tops.

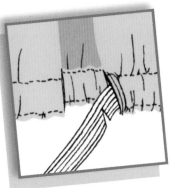

Elasticized Waist,
page 92

Side-Tied Drawstring Waist,
page 96

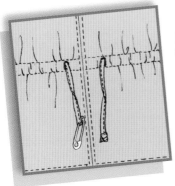

Front-Tied Drawstring Waist, page 100

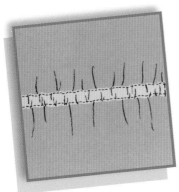

Partially Tunneled Elasticized Back, page 104

Elasticized Waist
Making the casing tunnel

1. Construct the jacket to the point at which you would insert the zipper. Then try on the jacket and mark the desired finished length—which will also be the position for the casing—with a row of pins or chalk marks.

2. To mark the fold line for the casing, connect the markings with a line of basting stitches. Remove any pins.

3. With the jacket wrong side out, trim to ¼ inch the vertical seam allowances of any seams below the basted fold line.

4. To determine the depth of the casing, add ½ inch to the width of the elastic you plan to use.

5. Measure down from the basting the distance determined in the previous step, and draw a chalk line around the edge.

6. Trim off the jacket edge along the chalk line.

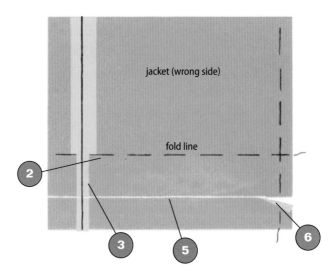

jacket (wrong side)

fold line

7. Fold up the bottom edge toward the wrong side of the jacket, along the bastings. Then baste along the fold.

8. Pin the top folded edge to the jacket at 1-inch intervals.

9. Baste the top edge to the jacket and remove the pins.

10. To complete the casing, machine stitch ⅛ inch from both folded edges. Remove the bastings.

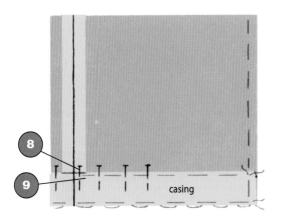

casing

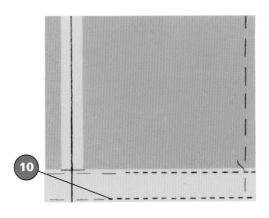

Elasticized Waist
Inserting the elastic

11. Without cutting the elastic to its final length, attach a small safety pin to one end. Then insert the pinned end of the elastic into one end of the casing, and work it through. Remove the pin.

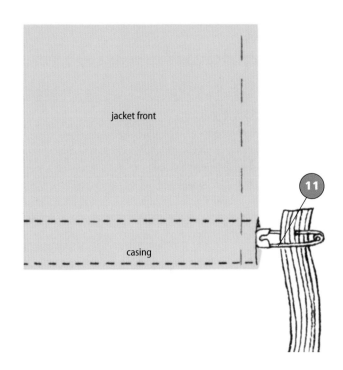

jacket front

casing

Select-*n*-Stitch FASHION ELEMENTS

12. Pin the elastic to the casing 1 to 1½ inches from the center-front seam line. Catch the elastic ½ inch from its end.

13. Make a vertical row of machine stitches across the casing, and remove the pin.

14. Try on the jacket, and stretch the elastic until it is secure and comfortable.

15. Pin the end of the elastic to the casing opening.

16. Make a row of machine stitches across the casing at a distance from its end equal to that used on the first side. Remove the pin.

17. Cut off the excess elastic ½ inch from the stitches.

18. Finish the jacket according to your pattern instructions.

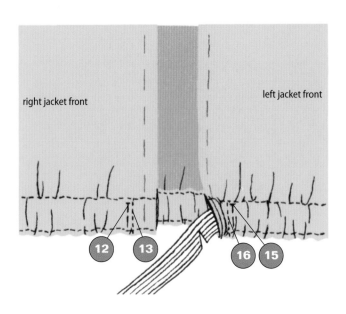

right jacket front

left jacket front

Side-Tied Drawstring Waist

Making the casing tunnel

1. Construct the jacket to the point at which you would insert the zipper. Then turn the jacket wrong side out—and make a line of basting stitches along the pattern markings for the casing fold line. If the pattern does not have a fold line, follow the instructions for the elasticized waist (*page 92, Steps 1–6*).

2. With the jacket wrong side out, trim to ¼ inch the seam allowances of any vertical seams below the bastings.

3. Fold the bottom edge ¼ inch. Press.

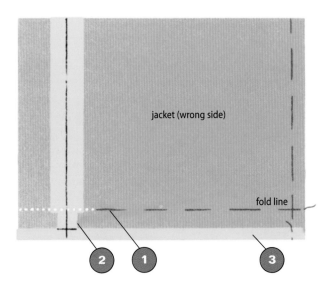

jacket (wrong side)

fold line

4. At the side seams, fold up the edge along the bastings, and place three or four pins in the jacket body just outside the folded edge. Do not catch the fold.

5. Turn the jacket wrong side down. To provide an opening for the drawstring, mark the position for eyelets between the bastings and the pins. Make a mark 1 inch from each side of each side seam.

6. Apply four large eyelets through the single outer jacket layer at the marks made in Step 5.

7. Complete the casing tunnel, following the instructions for the elasticized waist *(page 93, Steps 7–10)*.

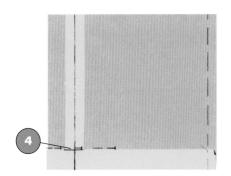

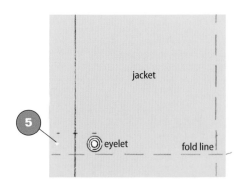

jacket

⊚ eyelet   fold line

Side-Tied Drawstring Waist
Making the drawstring

8a. If you are making the drawstring from garment fabric, cut out a strip of fabric on the grain—that is, parallel to either the lengthwise or the selvage edge. The strip should be twice the width of the casing between the two parallel rows of stitching, plus ¼ inch. The strip should be at least two times your waist measurement.

8b. If you are using a purchased drawstring, cut it so that it is the width of the casing and at least twice your waist measurement. Cut the drawstring in half. Cut one of the pieces in half again. Skip to Step 16.

9. By the same token, if the drawstring is to be made of garment fabric, cut the fabric in half. Then cut one of the pieces in half again.

10. On the long fabric piece, fold over ¼ inch at each short end toward the wrong side. Press.

11. Fold over the two lengthwise edges ¼ inch toward the wrong side. Pin at 1-inch intervals. Baste and remove the pins.

12. Fold the strip in half lengthwise with the folded edges inside. Pin the edges together at 1-inch intervals along the length of the strip. Baste and remove the pins.

13. Starting at the fold made in Step 10, machine stitch across one short end. Pivot and stitch as close to the long folded edges as possible. Then pivot and stitch across the other short end.

14. On the short fabric pieces, fold over ¼ inch at one short end and press.

15. To finish the short drawstring sections, repeat Steps 11–13, stitching only along the folded edges.

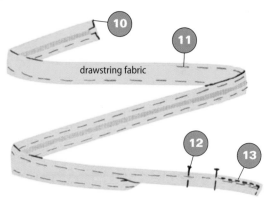

drawstring fabric

Inserting the drawstring

16. To thread one of the short drawstring pieces through the casing on one of the jacket front sections, first attach a safety pin to the stitched end of the drawstring. Then insert it into the casing at the center front, and work the drawstring through the casing until the safety pin emerges from the nearest eyelet. Remove the safety pin.

17. Pin the drawstring to the casing 1 to 1½ inches from the center-front seam line, catching the drawstring ½ inch from its end.

18. Machine stitch across the casing. Remove the pin.

19. At the eyelet end of the drawstring, tie a tight knot as close to the end of the drawstring as possible.

20. Repeat Steps 16–19 to thread the other short drawstring piece through the other jacket front.

21. To thread the remaining drawstring piece through the casing on the jacket back, repeat Step 16. This time insert the safety pin into one eyelet and bring it out through the other.

22. Tie a tight knot as close to each end of the drawstring as possible.

23. Finish the jacket according to the pattern instructions.

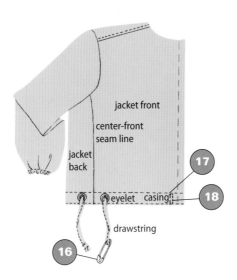

jacket front

center-front seam line

jacket back

eyelet casing

drawstring

Front-Tied Drawstring Waist
Making the casing

1. To provide a finished opening for the drawstring, mark the position for two vertical buttonholes, as indicated on the pattern. Then make a machine buttonhole at each mark, following the instructions provided with your sewing machine.

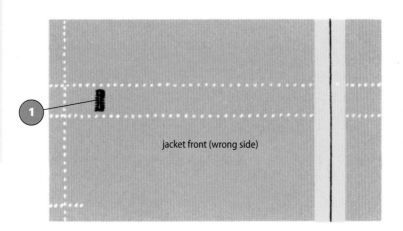

jacket front (wrong side)

2. Cut out the strip of fabric that will form the casing, using the pattern piece provided—or the measurements given in the pattern instruction guide. Alternately, on heavy fabric, cut a length of bias tape.

3. For a fabric casing, fold over each long edge ¼ inch. Then baste next to the fold. The bias tape can be sewed along its raw edges.

casing fabric (wrong side)

Front-Tied Drawstring Waist
Making the casing

4. With the jacket turned wrong side out, align the casing wrong side down over the waistline markings.

5. Pin both long edges of the casing to the jacket at 1-inch intervals, following the pattern markings on the jacket.

6. Baste the casing to the jacket along the long edges. Remove the pins.

7. Machine stitch the casing to the jacket ⅛ inch from the long edges. Remove all bastings.

8. Complete the jacket following the pattern instructions.

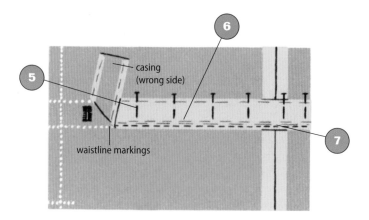

casing
(wrong side)

waistline markings

Inserting the drawstring

9. Make a drawstring following the instructions for the side-tied drawstring waist *(page 98, Steps 8–13)*, but make the drawstring only 1½ times your waist measurement, and do not cut it.

10. Attach a safety pin to one end of the drawstring, and insert the pin into one buttonhole. Then work the pin through the casing until the drawstring emerges from the other buttonhole. Remove the safety pin.

11. Tie a tight knot as close to each end of the drawstring as possible.

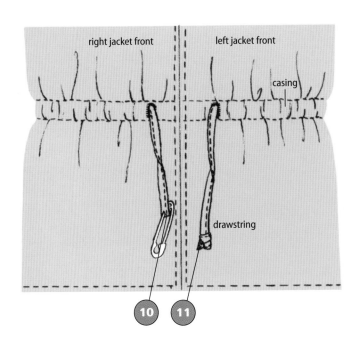

right jacket front

left jacket front

casing

drawstring

10 11

Partially Tunneled Elasticized Back
Making the casing

1. Make a casing and attach it to the unstitched jacket back section, following the instructions for the front-tied drawstring waist with a casing (*pages 101-102, Steps 2–7*).

2. Cut a length of elastic that is one third your waistline measurement, plus 1 inch.

3. Attach a safety pin to one end of the elastic. Then insert the pin into one end of the casing. Work the elastic through to the other end.

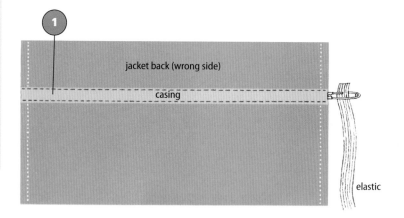

jacket back (wrong side)

casing

elastic

Finishing the casing

4. Pin both ends of the elastic to the casing at the side seam lines. Then remove the safety pin.

5. Make a vertical row of machine stitches across the ends of the casing within the seam allowance, and remove the pins.

6. Finish the jacket according to your pattern instructions.

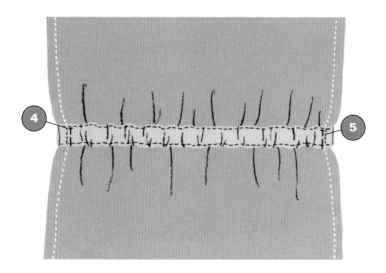

Appendix

Whether you're trying a new technique or remembering an old one, sometimes you need more details that the pattern instructions offer. Get the details right with these helpful methods for fitting and adjusting patterns. Plus, refresh your basic skills by reviewing useful stitches and sewing procedures.

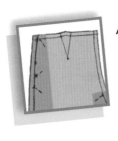

Buttons & Buttonholes 158

Basic Stitches 164

APPENDIX

Pants/Skirt: Letting Out the Waist

1. Produce more fabric around a tight-fitting skirt or pants waistline by first removing the waistband.

2. Rip out the side seams from the waistline to slightly below the bottom of the tight area. Then try on the garment, and turn the side seam allowances to one side.

3. Refold the turned-under seam allowances outside the original crease lines.

4. Pin the folded seam allowances to the flattened seam allowances so the garment fits the contours of your body and each side of the seam is let out equally.

5. Remove the garment and make a chalk mark at every pin on both sides of each seam. Remove the pins.

waistband

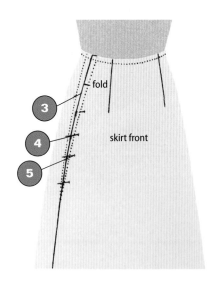

fold

skirt front

6. Turn the garment wrong side out. Pin the side seams together at the chalk marks, then baste and remove the pins.

7. Try on the garment and make any necessary fitting adjustments. Remove the garment.

8. Machine stitch each of the new side seams. Then remove the basting, and press the seam allowances open.

9. Reattach the waistband if it is long enough to accommodate the additional fullness released from the side seams. Otherwise, finish the waistline edge with grosgrain ribbon facings *(see pages 54–57).*

skirt front (wrong side)

Pants/Skirt: Taking In the Waist

1. Eliminate excess fabric from around the waistline of a loose-fitting skirt or pants by first removing the waistband.

2. Try on the garment and pin the side seams so the waistline of the garment aligns with your own and the sides fit the contours of your body.

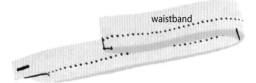

waistband

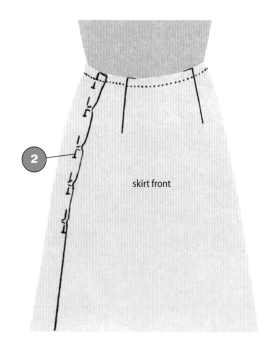

skirt front

3. Remove the garment and turn it wrong side out.

4. Make a chalk mark at every pin on one side of each seam. Remove the pins.

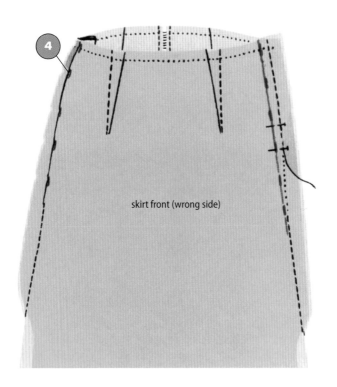

skirt front (wrong side)

Pants/Skirt: Taking In the Waist

5. Draw new side seams by connecting each set of the chalk marks with smooth lines that taper gradually into the original side seams.

6. Pin along the new side seam lines, then baste and remove the pins and the original line of stitching.

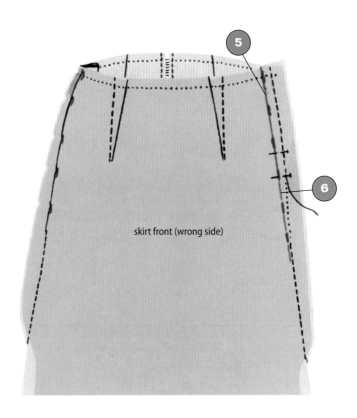

skirt front (wrong side)

7. Try on the garment and make any necessary fitting adjustments. Remove the garment.

8. Machine stitch each of the new side seams. Remove the basting.

9. Trim the new seam allowances to match the original seam allowances of the garment and press them open.

10. Shorten each end of the waistband by an amount equal to that taken out of each side seam. Then reattach the waistband to the garment.

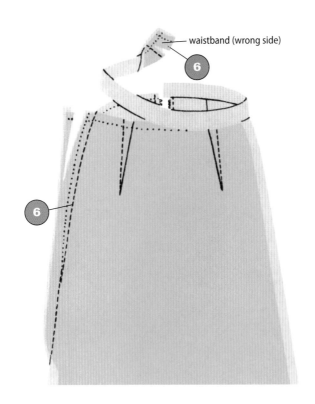

waistband (wrong side)

Pants/Skirt: Taking In a Back Waistline Bulge

1. Eliminate excess fabric from below the back waistline of a skirt or pants by first ripping out the back waistband from side seam to side seam.

2. Try on the garment and pin the waistband to the skirt or pants at the center back, far enough below the original attachment line to eliminate the bulge; place the waistband along the waistline contour of your body.

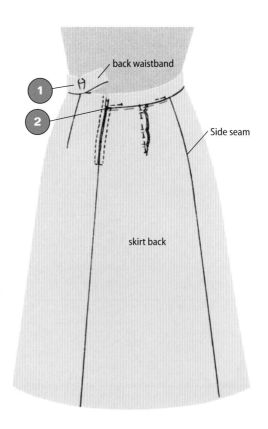

back waistband

Side seam

skirt back

3. Pin fit the back darts, lengthening and widening them to follow your body contours.

4. Remove the skirt. Mark the new waistband attachment line with a row of basting stitches along the skirt or pants, where the edge of the waistband meets them. Remove the waistband pins.

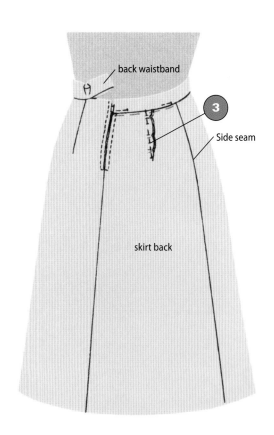

back waistband

3

Side seam

skirt back

Pants/Skirt: Taking In a Back Waistline Bulge

5. Baste in the new, longer darts: Turn the garment wrong side out, and use chalk to mark the location of each pin. Remove the pins. At each chalk mark, fold the garment, blending the new fold into the original dart fold. Pin the new fold. Starting several inches down from the tips of the dart seams, baste from the dart seams to the chalk marks. Remove the pins.

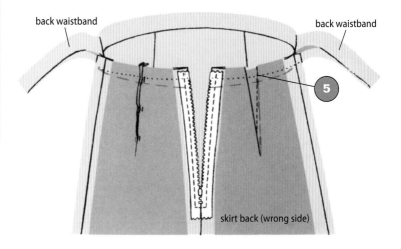

back waistband

back waistband

skirt back (wrong side)

5

6. Baste the waistband to the skirt or pants at the new waistband attachment line.

7. Try on the skirt or pants and make any necessary fitting adjustments. Remove the skirt.

8. Remove the basting attaching the waistband to the skirt or pants and stitch the darts. Then reattach the waistband as it was originally attached but in the new position.

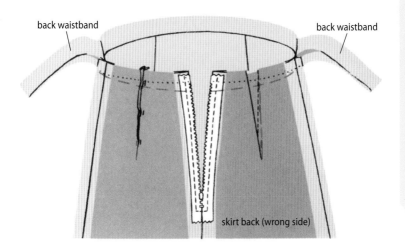

back waistband

back waistband

skirt back (wrong side)

Pants/Skirt: Taking In the Center Back

1. Eliminate extra fabric from the center of the pants back by first pinning the fabric at the waistband and along the back seam so the pants fit the contours of the body.

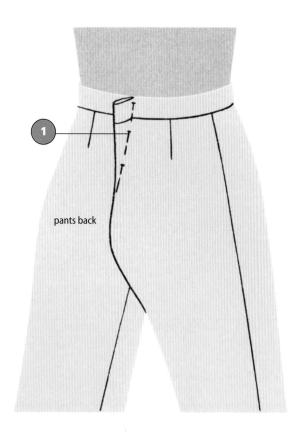

pants back

2. Remove the pants and turn them wrong side out. Make chalk marks at every pin on both sides of the waistband and center-back seam, then remove the pins.

3. Rip out the waistband for about 3 inches on each side of the center back. Then rip out the center-back seam to just below the chalk marks.

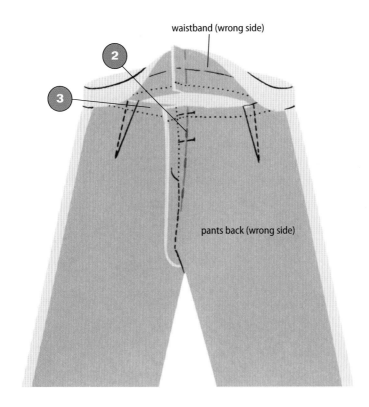

waistband (wrong side)

pants back (wrong side)

Pants/Skirt: Taking In the Center Back

4. Cut the waistband in half at the center back. Baste a new center-back seam in the waistband by aligning the cut edges and using the chalk marks as a guide. Press the seam allowance open.

5. Draw a new center-back seam on the pants by connecting the chalk marks made in Step 2 with a smooth line that tapers gradually into the original seam.

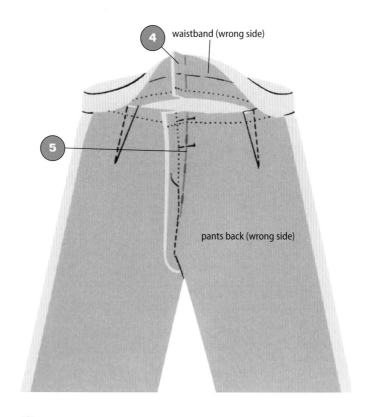

waistband (wrong side)

pants back (wrong side)

6. Pin along the chalk line, then baste and remove the pins.

7. Baste the waistband to the pants along the original waistline seam. Then try on the garment and make any necessary fitting adjustments. Remove the garment, and remove the basting attaching the waistband to the pants.

8. Machine stitch the new center-back seam on the pants and the waistband, and remove the basting. Trim the seam allowances and press them open.

9. Reattach the waistband.

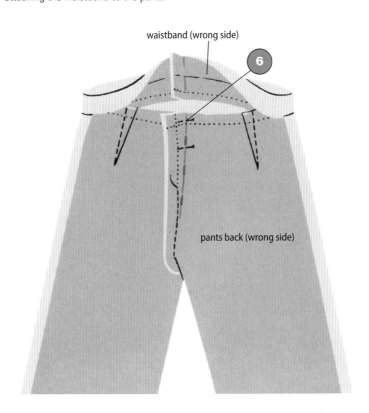

waistband (wrong side)

pants back (wrong side)

Dress: Lower Back Is Too Long

Symptoms of the lower back that is too long

1. Crosswise wrinkles appear just below the waist in the back of the skirt.

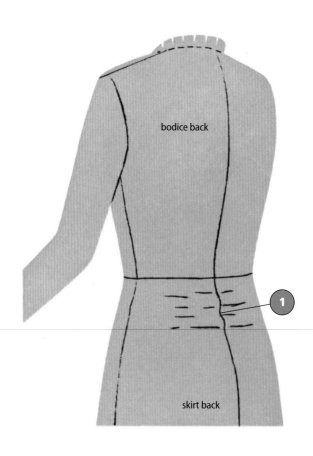

bodice back

1

skirt back

Refitting the skirt back

2. Starting in the center back of the skirt just below your waistline, pinch the excess fabric between thumb and index finger into, a horizontal tuck. Insert a pin at the base of the tuck.

3. Extend the tuck to both side seams, tapering it to a point on each side and inserting pins as you do so. Take off the muslin.

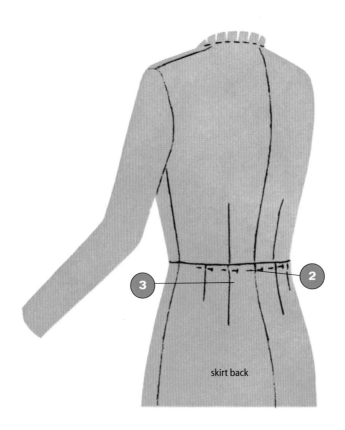

skirt back

Dress: Lower Back Is Too Long
Refitting the skirt back

4. Measure along the center back seam line of the skirt from the pin inserted in Step 2 to the top edge of the tuck. Multiply the measurement by two.

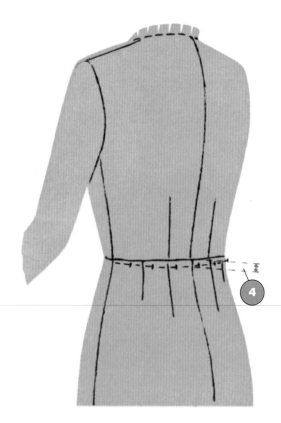

124 Select-*n*-Stitch FASHION ELEMENTS

APPENDIX: ADJUSTING PATTERNS

Adjusting the pattern

5. With the ruler at a right angle to the center back seam line on the skirt back pattern, draw a line from the intersection of the waist seam line and the center back seam line to the side seam line.

6. Measure down the center back seam line from the waist seam line the distance calculated in Step 4 and mark

with a dot. Draw a line from the dot to the intersection of the line made in Step 5 and the side seam line.

7. Fold the pattern piece along the line made in Step 6, then turn the folded edge up to coincide with the line made in Step 5, forming a tuck that is wide at the center back and tapers to a point at the side. Pin the tuck flat. Re-draw the dart seam lines over the tuck.

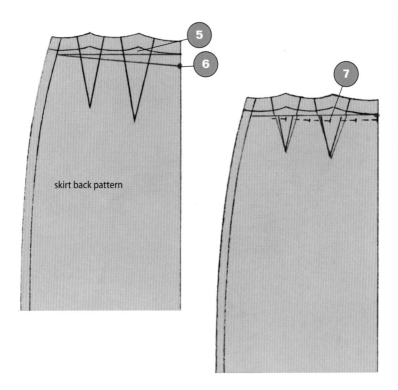

skirt back pattern

Dress: Skirt Front Is Tight

Symptoms of a tight skirt front

1. The skirt feels snug across your abdomen.

2. Wrinkles radiate from the abdomen toward the side seams.

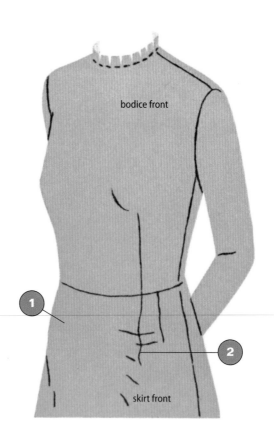

bodice front

skirt front

Refitting the skirt front

3. Open the front waist seam from one side seam to the other.

4. Slide the skirt front down away from the bodice until the wrinkles below the darts disappear.

5. Starting from the center front and tapering evenly into the original waist seam line toward the sides, pin the seam allowance of the skirt waist to the bodice waist seam line.

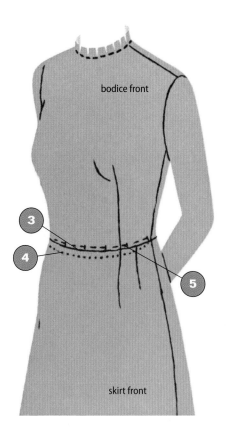

bodice front

skirt front

Dress: Skirt Front Is Tight
Refitting the skirt front

6. Open the skirt front darts and shorten the darts until all wrinkles disappear. Insert pins end to end along the base of each dart, Take off the muslin.

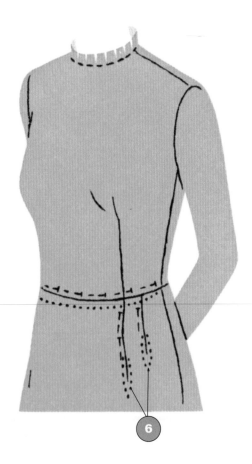

7. At the center front of the skirt, measure from the new waist seam line to the original one.

8. Measure the length of each shortened dart.

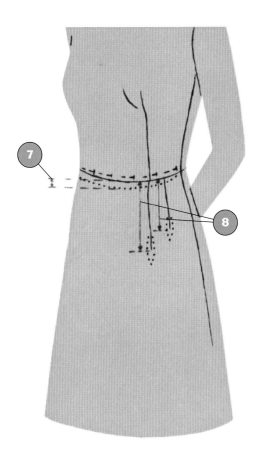

Dress: Skirt Front Is Tight
Adjusting the pattern

9. On the skirt front pattern, draw a line at a right angle to the center front line from the intersection of the center line and the waist seam line to the side seam line. Cut along the pencil line to the side seam line but do not cut the pattern apart.

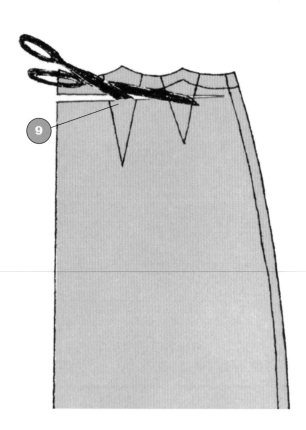

10. Slide an insert of shelf paper under the slash and spread the sections of the pattern apart at the center line to the distance measured in Step 7 and pin them to the shelf paper.

11. Draw a line to connect the original center front line of the two edges. Trim away excess shelf paper.

12. On both original darts, measure down the center from the waist seam line a distance equal to that measured in Step 8 and mark with dots.

13. Draw new seam lines from the dots made in Step 12 to the base of the original darts at the waist seam line.

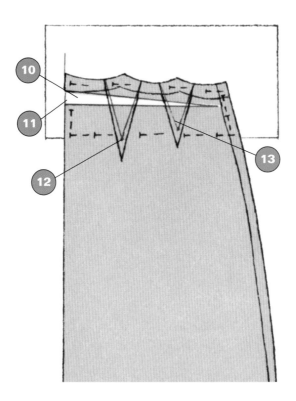

Pants/Skirt: Loose at the Side Seam

Symptoms of a loose waist, hip, or leg

1. The pants stand away from your body at the waist, hip, or leg.

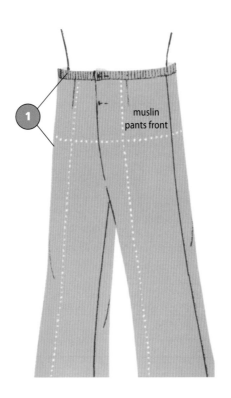

muslin
pants front

Tucking the side seam

2. Remove the waistband and, on the point of the side seam that is widest, pinch the excess fabric into a vertical tuck, then pin.

3. Continue to tuck and pin the excess fabric down the length of the side seam. Taper it into the original seam at mid-hip for the waist correction, or taper it into the original seam above and below the leg or hip correction until the pants fit comfortably.

4. If the leg adjustment is insufficient, tuck the excess fabric on the inseam, starting at the crotch. Taper it into the original seam just above the knee.

5. Measure and mark the adjusted seam or seams (*pages 150–157*).

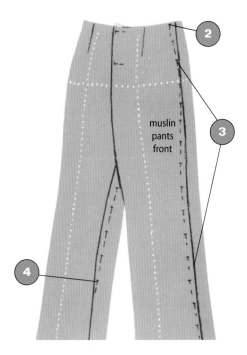

muslin
pants
front

Pants/Skirt: Loose at the Side Seam
Adjusting the pattern

6. On the side seam of the pants-front pattern piece at the waist, measure the depth of the widest point of the muslin correction from the original to the adjusted seam allowance. Mark with a dot inside the seam allowance.

7. Measure the length of the muslin correction from the widest point to the tapered point. Mark with a dot on the seam line. Then, to make the new side seam, join the dots following the curve of the original seam.

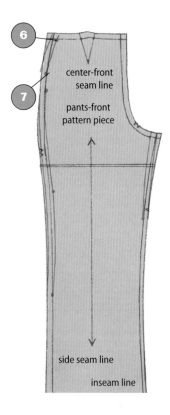

center-front seam line

pants-front pattern piece

side seam line

inseam line

8. Draw a new cutting line ⅝ inch outside the new seam line and parallel to it.

9. On the hip or leg of the pants, repeat Steps 6–8, tapering the adjustment into the original side seam above and below the hip or leg correction.

10. Measure the width of the muslin crotch correction at its widest point. Mark with a dot inside the seam line on the inseam.

11. Measure the length of the muslin crotch correction. Mark with a dot on the inseam line. Then, join the dots to make the new inseam stitching line and repeat Step 8 to make the new cutting line.

12. Repeat Steps 6–11 on the pants-back pattern piece.

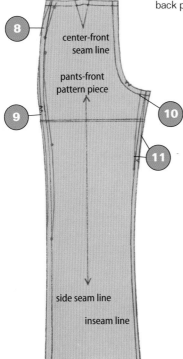

center-front
seam line

pants-front
pattern piece

side seam line

inseam line

Pants/Skirt: Tight at the Side Seam

Symptoms of a tight waist, hip, or leg

1. If the pants are tight at the waist, they feel snug at the waist and wrinkles form under the waistband.

2. If the pants are tight in the hip or leg, they feel snug and wrinkles form at the inseam and outseam.

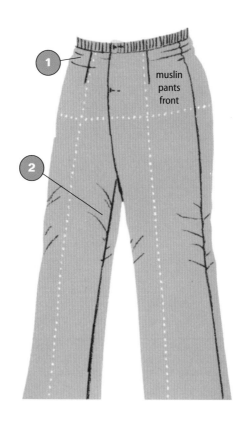

muslin
pants
front

Letting out the side seam

3. Remove the waistband and open both side seams in the area that is snug.

4. Partially unfold each seam allowance until the pants are smooth and comfortable at each side. Pin the adjustment.

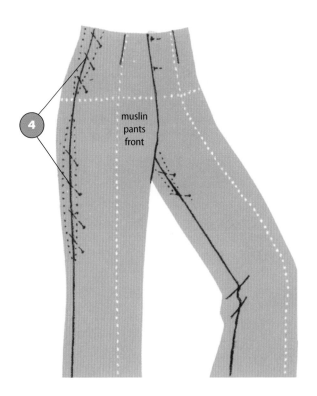

4

muslin
pants
front

Pants/Skirt: Tight at the Side Seam
Symptoms of a tight waist, hip, or leg

5. If the leg adjustment is insufficient, open the inseam from the crotch midway to the knee and repeat Step 4.

6. Taper the adjustment into the original seam, inserting pins as you go.

7. Mark and measure the adjusted seam *(pages 150–157)*.

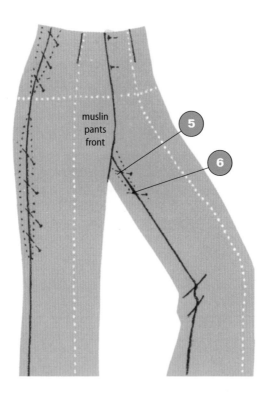

muslin pants front

Adjusting the pattern

8. On the side seam of the pants-front pattern piece, measure at the waist the width of the muslin correction at its widest point from the original to the adjusted seam. Mark with a dot outside the side seam line.

9. Measure the length of the muslin correction from the widest point to the tapered point or points. Mark with a dot on the seam line and join the dots following the curve of the original seam to make the new side seam.

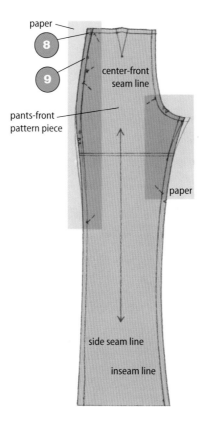

paper

8

9

center-front
seam line

pants-front
pattern piece

paper

side seam line

inseam line

Pants/Skirt: Tight at the Side Seam
Adjusting the pattern

10. Pin a piece of paper to the pattern piece in the adjusted area and draw a new cutting line ⅝ inch outside the new seam line and parallel to it.

11. To adjust the hip or leg, repeat Steps 8–10, tapering the correction into the original side seam above and below the correction.

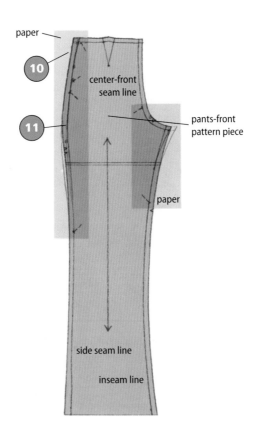

paper

center-front seam line

pants-front pattern piece

paper

side seam line

inseam line

12. Measure the width of the muslin crotch correction. Mark with a dot outside the seam line on the inseam of the pattern piece.

13. Measure the length of the muslin crotch correction. Mark with a dot on the inseam line. Then join the dots,

following the curve of the original seam to make the new crotch seam.

14. To draw a new cutting line, repeat Step 10.

15. Repeat Steps 8–14 on the pants-back pattern piece.

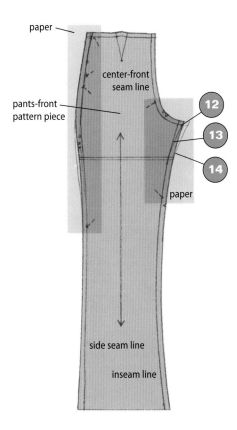

paper

center-front seam line

pants-front pattern piece

12

13

14

paper

side seam line

inseam line

Pants/Skirt: Tight at the Hipbone

Symptoms of tight upper hip

1. The pants feel snug across the hipbone and wrinkles radiate out from the side seams.

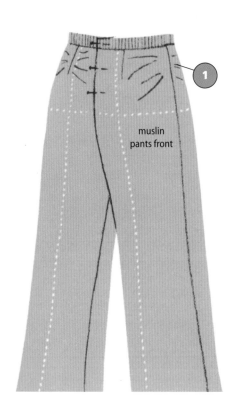

muslin
pants front

Letting out the hipline

2. Open both side seams from the waist to the hip.

3. Starting at the waist, smooth the pants front and back together until they meet comfortably at each side.

4. Unfold enough of the pants-front seam allowance to overlap the back seam allowance. Pin the fold outside the original seam-allowance markings. Let out more fabric in the front than in the back seam allowance if necessary.

5. Taper the adjusted seam into the original seam, inserting pins as you go.

6. Open the front darts, and repin to fit the contours of the body.

7. Mark and measure the adjusted side seam and the dart (*pages 150–157*).

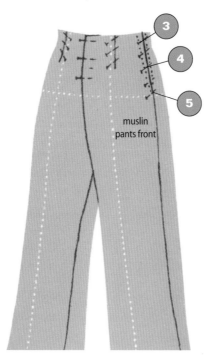

muslin
pants front

Pants/Skirt: Tight at the Hipbone

Adjusting the pattern

8. On the waistline of the pants-front pattern piece, measure the width of the muslin correction from the original to the adjusted seam. Mark with a dot at the side seam.

9. Measure on the side seam the length from the waistline to the tapered point of the muslin correction. Mark the length of the adjustment with a dot on the seam line. Then join the dots with a line following the curve of the original seam to make the new side seam.

10. Pin a piece of paper on the side seam, and draw a new cutting line ⅝ inch outside the new seam line and parallel to it.

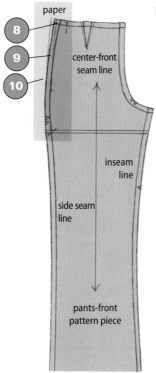

paper

center-front
seam line

inseam
line

side seam
line

pants-front
pattern piece

11. Repeat Steps 8–10 on the pants-back pattern piece.

12. Distribute the amount of the dart adjustment from the muslin correction on both sides of the original dart markings. Mark with a dot on the outside of the original dart markings at the waistline.

13. Taper a line from each dot to a point below the original point of the dart.

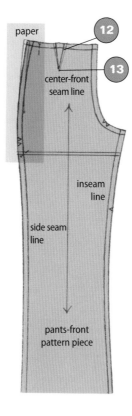

Pants/Skirt: Back Waist Is High

Symptoms of a high waist

1. The pants waist is higher than the natural waistline.

2. Horizontal folds form under the waistband at the pants back.

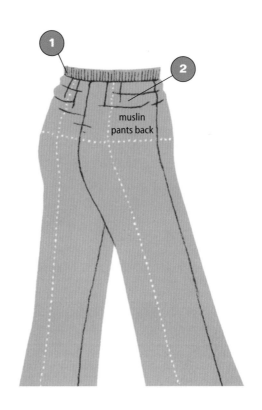

muslin
pants back

Tucking the back

3. Starting at the center back of the pants about 3 inches below the waist, pinch the excess fabric into a horizontal tuck, and pin.

4. Extend the tuck to both side seams, tapering it to a point on each side; pin as you go.

5. Mark and measure the tuck *(page 150)*.

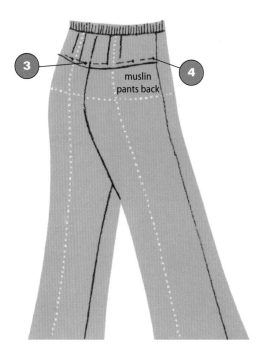

muslin
pants back

Pants/Skirt: Back Waist Is High
Adjusting the pattern

6. On the center-back seam of the pants-back pattern piece, measure from the waistline to the top of the tucked muslin adjustment. Mark with a dot.

7. Draw a line from the dot made in Step 6 straight across to the side seam.

8. Measure the depth of the tucked muslin correction from the dot made in Step 6 down the center-back seam line. Mark with a dot.

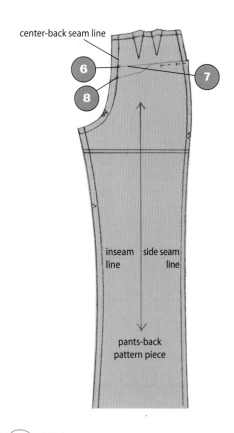

center-back seam line

inseam
line

side seam
line

pants-back
pattern piece

9. Draw a tapering line from the dot made in Step 8 to the point where the line made in Step 7 intersects the side seam.

10. Fold the pattern along the line made in Step 9, and turn the folded edge over so that it meets the line made in Step 7, forming a tuck that tapers to a point at the side seam. Pin the tuck flat.

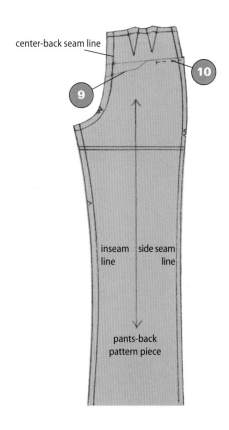

center-back seam line

inseam line

side seam line

pants-back pattern piece

Marking and Measuring Muslin Adjustments

If the muslin was tucked

1. Baste the tuck along its base and remove the pins. Then baste the tuck flat.

2. Measure the depth of the tuck at its widest point.

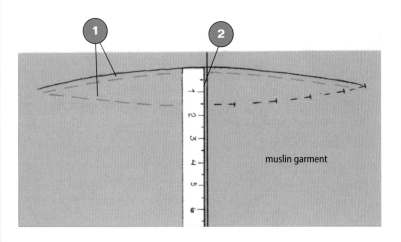

muslin garment

If the muslin was slashed

1. Place the muslin wrong side down. Baste the muslin insert to the garment fabric along the cut edges of the slash; remove the pins.

2. Measure the depth of the slashed adjustment at its widest point.

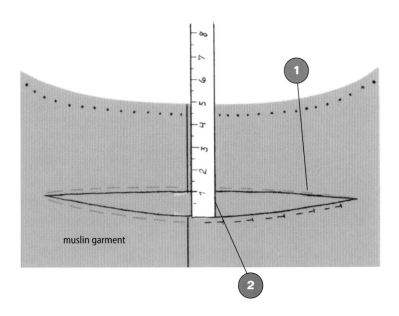

muslin garment

Marking and Measuring Muslin Adjustments

If the muslin was tucked at a seam

1. Turn the muslin wrong side out and fold the garment along the tucked seam.

2. With your fingers, locate the pins along the folded line of the muslin. Mark this position with chalk.

3. Mark the beginning and end of the tuck with chalk lines at right angles to the seam line.

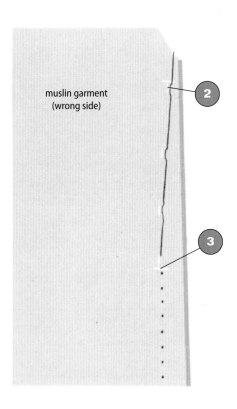

muslin garment
(wrong side)

4. Unpin the tuck to make the new seam line; connect the chalk marks made in Step 2.

5. Measure the tuck at its widest point, from the original seam marking to the adjusted seam line.

6. Measure the length of the tuck from end to end.

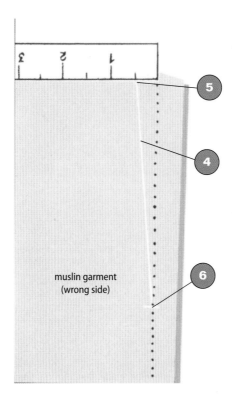

muslin garment
(wrong side)

Marking and Measuring Muslin Adjustments

If the muslin seam was let out

1. Mark both edges of the pinned seam along the fold with chalk lines at 2-inch intervals.

2. Mark the ends of the adjusted seam with chalk lines at right angles to the seam line.

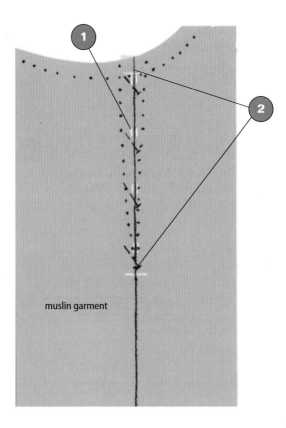

muslin garment

3. Unpin the seam and open the seam 1 inch below the end of the correction. Connect the chalk marks with a smooth line, tapering the line into the original seam line.

4. Measure the width of the adjustment at its widest point, from the original to the adjusted seam line.

5. Measure the length of the adjustment from end to end.

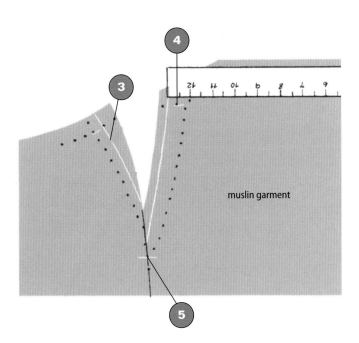

muslin garment

Marking and Measuring Muslin Adjustments

If the muslin seam was taken in

1. Mark both edges of the pinned seam
with chalk lines at 1-inch intervals.

muslin garment

2. Mark the ends of the adjusted seam with chalk lines at right angles to the seam line.

3. To complete marking and measuring the adjustment, repeat Steps 3–5 for letting out the seam. Mark inside the original seam allowance.

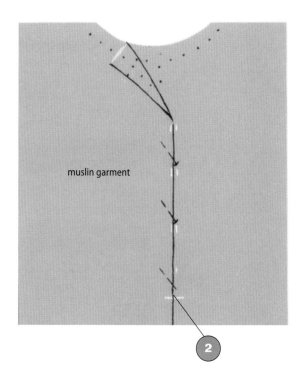

muslin garment

2

Measuring the Button

To find the size of your buttonholes, first measure the buttons to be attached. For a flat, thin button, measure its diameter and add ⅛ inch. For a thicker button, measure its diameter and add ¼ inch. For a mounded or ball button, place a thin strip of paper across the mound or ball, pin it tightly in place, slide the paper off, flatten it, then measure it and add ¼ inch.

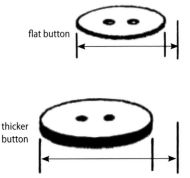

flat button

thicker button

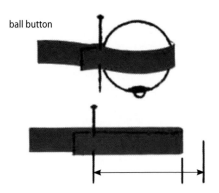

ball button

Buttonhole Stitch

1. Using a knotted thread, insert the needle from the wrong side of the fabric ⅛ inch down from the top edge.

2. Form a loop with the thread by swinging it around in a circle counterclockwise.

3. Insert the needle from the wrong side of the fabric through the same point at which the needle emerged in Step 1, keeping the looped thread under the needle.

4. Draw the thread through, firmly pulling it straight up toward the top edge of the fabric.

5. Repeat Steps 2–4 directly to the left of the first stitch, and continue to make close stitches of even length, forming a firm ridge along the top. End with a fastening stitch *(page 166)* on the wrong side of the fabric.

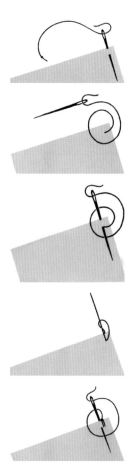

Making the Buttonhole

1a. To make a buttonhole entirely by machine, follow the instructions provided with your particular model.

1b. To make a buttonhole without a special accessory, begin halfway between the placement lines and sew tiny machine stitches ⅟₁₆ inch outside the running stitches that mark the buttonhole position. The stitches should be continuous, pivoting at the corners.

2. With a small pointed scissors, cut the buttonhole along the running stitches, starting in the middle and cutting to each placement line.

3. Sew the buttonhole edges with overcast stitches *(page 168)*, shown in black, to protect them from fraying.

4. Work the overcast edges with a buttonhole stitch *(page 159)*, beginning on the top edge of the buttonhole at the inner placement line.

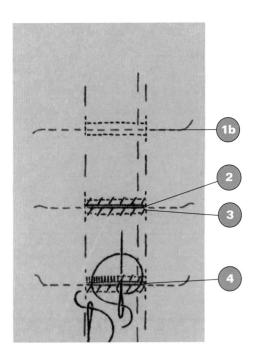

5. At the outer placement line, make five to seven long buttonhole stitches, fanning out about ¹⁄₁₆ inch beyond the line. Then turn the garment around and repeat for the lower edge. End with a straight vertical stitch at the inner placement line.

6. To finish off the inner edge of the buttonhole with a reinforcement called a bar tack, make three long stitches, side by side, from the top to the bottom edge of the completed rows of buttonhole stitches. These stitches should extend ¹⁄₁₆ inch beyond the inner placement line.

7. At the bottom edge of the buttonhole, insert the needle horizontally under the three straight stitches made in Step 6, catching the top layer of the fabric underneath. Then pull the needle through, keeping the thread under the needle.

8. Continue to make small stitches across the three long stitches the full depth of the buttonhole.

9. End with two small fastening stitches (page 166).

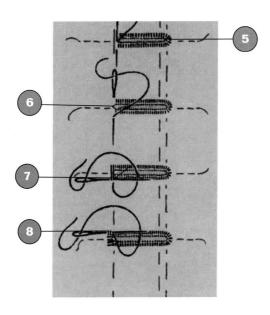

Sewing on Buttons with Holes

1. Using a strand of knotted buttonhole twist, make a small stitch in the fabric at the point where the center of the button is to fall. Insert the needle through one of the holes on the underside of the button and pull the thread through.

2. Hold a wooden kitchen match or a toothpick between the button holes and pull the thread over it as you point the needle down into the other hole. Then make two or three stitches across the match; in the case of a four-hole button, make two rows of parallel stitches across the match.

3. Remove the match and pull the button up, away from the fabric, to the top of the threads.

4. Wind the thread five or six times, tightly, around the loose threads below the button to create a thread shank.

5. End by making a fastening stitch (*page 166*) in the thread shank.

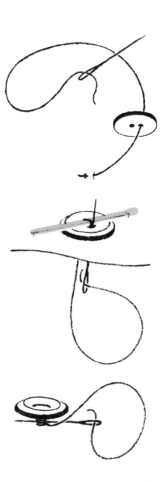

Sewing on Buttons with Shanks

1. Using a strand of knotted buttonhole twist, make a small stitch in the fabric at the point where the center of the button is to fall. Insert the needle through the hole in the shank of the button and pull the thread through.

2. Angle the button away from the fabric with your thumb and take two or three stitches through the button shank.

3. Wind the thread tightly five or six times around the thread shank made in Step 2.

4. End by making a fastening stitch *(page 166)* in the thread shank.

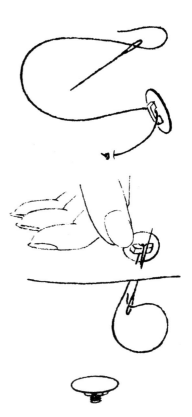

Basting Stitch

Insert the needle, with knotted thread, from the wrong side of the fabric and weave the needle in and out of the fabric several times in ⅛-inch, evenly spaced stitches. Pull the thread through. Continue across, making several stitches at a time, and end with a fastening stitch. When basting, make longer stitches, evenly spaced.

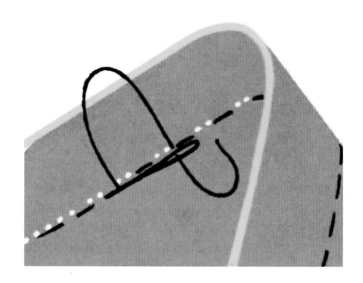

Catch Stitch

Working from left to right, anchor the first stitch with a knot inside the hem ¼ inch down from the edge. Point the needle to the left and pick up one or two threads on the garment directly above the hem, then pull the thread through. Take a small stitch in the hem only (not in the garment), ¼ inch down from the edge and ¼ inch to the right of the previous stitch. End with a fastening stitch.

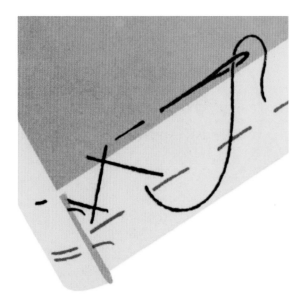

Fastening Stitch

After the last stitch, insert the needle back ¼ inch and bring it out at the point at which the thread last emerged. Make another stitch through these same points for extra firmness. To begin a row with a fastening stitch, leave a 4-inch loose end and make the initial stitch the same way as an ending stitch.

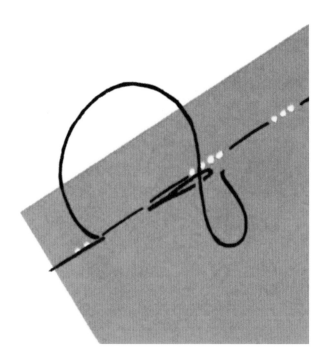

Hemming Stitch

Anchor the first stitch with a knot inside the hem; then pointing the needle up and to the left, pick up one or two threads of the garment fabric close to the hem. Push the needle up through the hem ⅛ inch above the edge; pull the thread through. Continue picking up one or two threads and making ⅛-inch stitches in the hem at intervals of ¼ inch. End with a fastening stitch.

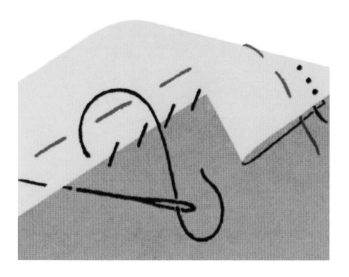

Overcast Stitch

Draw the needle, with knotted thread, through from the wrong side of the fabric ⅛ to ¼ inch down from the top edge. With the thread to the right, insert the needle under the fabric from the wrong side ⅛ to ¼ inch to the left of the first stitch. Continue to make evenly spaced stitches over the fabric edge and end with a fastening stitch.

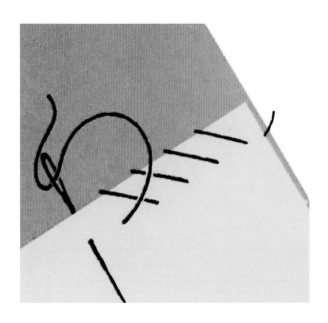

Slip Stitch

Fold under the hem edge and anchor the first stitch with a knot inside the fold. Point the needle to the left. Pick up one or two threads of the garment fabric close to the hem edge, directly below the first stitch, and slide the needle horizontally through the folded edge of the hem ⅛ inch to the left of the previous stitch. End with a fastening stitch.

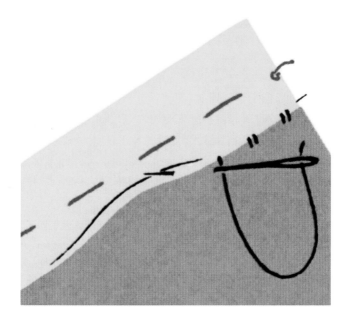

Index

Index

INDEX

Index

INDEX

Select-*n*-Stitch FASHION ELEMENTS
SERIES

A sexy slit skirt, distinguished French cuffs, or perfectly pleated trousers...
It's the specific elements of design that define the style and quality of a
garment. Each *Select-n-Stitch Fashion Elements* book provides a visual
directory to the many choices and techniques available when selecting
pockets, sleeves, collars and more to perfectly enhance a garment.

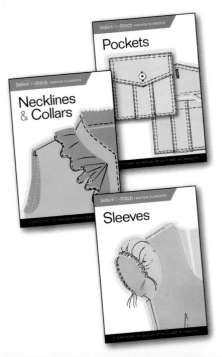

Pockets
ISBN: 978-1-56523-553-3
$12.95 • 152 Pages

Necklines & Collars
ISBN: 978-1-56523-572-4
$12.95 • 200 Pages

Sleeves
ISBN: 978-1-56523-571-7
$12.95 • 160 Pages

Look for These Books at Your Local Book or Craft Store

To order direct, call **800-457-9112 or** visit *www.FoxChapelPublishing.com*

By mail, please send check or money order + $4.00 per book for S&H to:
Fox Chapel Publishing, 1970 Broad Street, East Petersburg, PA 17520